EARLY CHILDHOOD EDUCATION SERIES

Leslie R. Williams, Editor

ADVISORY BOARD: Barbara T. Bowman, Harriet K. Cuffaro, Stephanie Feeney,
Doris Pronin Fromberg, Celia Genishi, Stacie G. Goffin, Dominic F. Gullo,
Alice Sterling Honig, Elizabeth Jones, Gwen Morgan, David Weikart

(Continued)

Let's Be Friends

*Peer Competence
and
Social Inclusion in
Early Childhood Programs*

KRISTEN MARY KEMPLE

foreword by
Mary Renck Jalongo

Teachers College
Columbia University
New York and London

Published by Teachers College Press, 1234 Amsterdam Avenue, New York, NY 10027

Chapter opening art by: Su-si (Chapters 1, 3, and 5); Nicholas (Chapters 2, 6, 7, and Epilogue); and Rachel (Chapter 4).

Library of Congress Cataloging-in-Publication Data

Kemple, Kristen Mary.
    Let's be friends : peer competence and social inclusion in early childhood programs /
Kristen Mary Kemple ; foreword by Mary Renck Jalongo.
       p. cm. — (Early childhood education series)
    Includes bibliographical references and index.
    ISBN 0-8077-4396-8 (cloth. : alk. paper) — ISBN 0-8077-4395-X (paper. : alk. paper)
       1. Socialization.   2. Social interaction in children—Study and teaching (Early
childhood)   3. Childhood with social disabilities—Education (Early childhood)   I. Title.
II. Early childhood education series (Teachers College Press)
LC192.4.K43 2003
371.9'046—dc22   2003060041

ISBN 0-8077-4395-X (paper)
ISBN 0-8077-4396-8 (cloth)

Printed on acid-free paper

Manufactured in the United States of America

11   10   09   08   07   06   05   04   8   7   6   5   4   3   2   1

For Nicholas and Alisaar.
May you always know the comfort of friendship.
May you always be friends.
I love you.

May 12, 2002
Mother's Day

Contents

Foreword

TEACHING'S MOST deeply affecting moments, both negative and positive, frequently focus on the relationships of children with their peers. Ranging from cruelty to compassion, it is the interpersonal dynamic, even more than the academic agenda, that shapes and defines young children's perceptions of school. The recognition that friendship is a critically important aspect in establishing a classroom community affects early childhood professionals from their earliest days in the classroom.

I vividly recall a student named Julie from my second group of first graders who was seriously injured in an auto accident and returned to school after an extended absence, ashamed of her facial scars and the irreversible damage to her hand. As the children lined up for recess, a peer contemptuously said, "Julie lost two fingers—ha, ha ha!" The damage caused by this boy's remark was staggering. I was powerless to counteract such hurtful words. Yet, when I took the child aside and angrily demanded, "What is wrong with you? Can't you see that you hurt Julie's feelings?" his puzzled reaction made it clear that he had been thoughtlessly rather than deliberately mean.

On my first day as a first-grade teacher, I met Russell, a boy in my class who had suffered a traumatic brain injury during infancy. The accident had caused one side of his body to atrophy while the other continued to grow and, and as a result the strong side was used to propel the shortened and withered arm and leg around. My idea for an activity to introduce everyone was something that I had seen many times before. I would trace the outline of the children's bodies on large paper and they would use markers and crayons to decorate the shape to represent their appearance. My heart sank when I saw Russell's unbalanced figure alongside the symmetrical outlines of his peers. I had unwittingly put him in an awkward situation, but I lacked the flexibility, imagination, and experience to modify my lesson plan on such short notice. So, I pushed on uneasily, asking each child to dictate a story to accompany their drawing. When it was Russell's turn, the six-year-old spoke these unforgettable words: "My name is Russell. I am a boy. I like myself and God loves me. If someone needs help, I will help them." Russell was true to these words. In fact, contrary to my fear that Russell might be ridiculed by peers, this young boy's kindness and joyfulness made him the most popular child in my class. On numerous occasions, I had to break up arguments in the lunchroom about who would have the privilege of sitting next to him. Yet I cannot take the credit for Russell's warm acceptance by peers in an era that antedated inclusion or even mainstreaming. What would I have done, I still wonder, if my worst fears about Russell had been realized?

This is what Kristen Kemple's book is all about. It is about building a repertoire of strategies that make the ideals of inclusion a reality. Her book is predicated on the assumption that genuine inclusion cannot exist unless every child is successfully integrated into the peer culture of the classroom. As you read, you will sense that you are in the presence of a thoughtful and knowledgeable guide who not only understands the critical role that early childhood educators play in promoting peer acceptance among the very young but also the profound and enduring consequences of peer relationships for children's development. Our author tells us that the book is "a call for simultaneous nurturing of individuality and groupness" but, like all effective teachers, she does more than tell. She shows us. Hers is a book that is richly populated with young children, their words, their concerns, and a host of collaborative strategies for promoting peer affirmation. How I wish that I had known everything in this book from my earliest days of teaching Russell and his classmates. How I wish that all young children would have had the benefit of teachers who read, understood, and implemented the ideas in this book. Above all, how I hope that my contemporaries who are pushing for a single-minded focus on academic achievement would embrace this message: that the promise of inclusion, indeed the promise of education, cannot be fulfilled by ignoring the social and emotional lives of learners.

Mary Renck Jalongo

Preface

PROMOTING CHILDREN'S healthy social development has traditionally been a central purpose of early childhood education. Establishment of friendships and growth of competence in social interaction are widely recognized as important contributions of early education. The purpose of this book is to describe methods of support and intervention that teachers can use to help create social inclusion in preschool and the primary grades. I have drawn on the practical and research literatures of both early childhood education and early childhood special education to present a wide variety of strategies to help children establish friendships and develop competence in peer interaction. Principles and approaches are shown through many illustrations based upon observations in preschool and primary classrooms.

This book uses two conceptual frameworks to help early childhood professionals manage the wide range of methods offered by the two early childhood disciplines. The framework of reflective teaching is described as a means of making reasoned choices about strategies likely to succeed in achieving specific outcomes for individual children in particular circumstances. The framework of collaborative teaming among professionals is also presented as a vehicle for making optimum use of the particular areas of expertise offered by various professionals concerned with early childhood development and education. Throughout the book, readers are encouraged to consider approaches along a continuum of most "normalized" or naturalistic to most directive and intense. The less directive, more natural interventions are often sufficient. Sometimes more intensive, direct, and less normalized interventions are warranted. In these cases, the more naturalistic strategies often serve as an important foundation that provides the undergirding for more intensive interventions.

Let's Be Friends is organized into seven chapters. Chapter 1 defines peer competence, describes its importance, and outlines the role of the early childhood teacher in promoting competent peer interaction. Chapter 2 describes similarities and differences in the perspectives and approaches of early childhood education and early childhood special education, and presents the utility of reflective teaching and professional collaboration as uni-fying frameworks to aid in selection of appropriate interventions.

Support and intervention strategies are described in Chapters 3 through 7. Chapter 3 focuses on setting the stage for peer interaction through purpose-ful arrangement of the physical, temporal, and socioemotional environment of the program. This chapter includes methods of arranging furniture, materi-als, and equipment to encourage and support competence in peer interaction; creation of social grouping arrangements; and ways of arranging time, sched-ules, and routines to support children's peer relationships and interactions.

Chapters 4 and 5 describe naturalistic strategies for promoting peer interaction. Chapter 4 includes the approaches of on-the-spot teaching and conflict mediation in the course of natural social interaction. Chapter 5 describes the use of planned small- and large-group learning experiences such as cooperative learning, literature and song sharing, puppetry, group affection activities, and group discussion.

In Chapter 6, high intensity coaching and training interventions are described. These approaches are sometimes needed when more naturalistic approaches have been deemed insufficient. The use of prompting and rein-forcement are considered, and incorporation of these in peer-mediated and teacher-mediated interventions is discussed.

Chapter 7 describes common needs and interventions for children ex-periencing specific challenges and disabilities. Methods of support and in-tervention are described that can be particularly useful for children with aggressive behavior patterns, children who are often shy, children with au-tism spectrum disorders, children with visual impairment, and children with hearing impairment.

The frameworks of reflective teaching and professional collaboration are carried throughout the book, and are central in the "Food for Thought" exer-cises at the end of each chapter. These exercises are designed to help readers reflect upon and apply what they read, and are grounded in respect for profes-sional teachers as informed and thoughtful decision makers.

An epilogue is included to remind readers of the role of community and collaboration as contexts and processes for promoting social compe-tence, and as potential outcomes of socially competent interaction. Parallels are drawn between the community of children and adults in the classroom, and the community of collaborating professionals who work to address the social needs of those young children.

The book concludes with two appendices. Appendix A is a listing of children's books about friendship and friendship skills. Appendix B is a listing of recorded songs for children that address social topics. Both ap-pendices correspond to suggested practices in Chapter 5, for using music and literature as teaching tools and as springboards for the discussion of friendship and other social topics.

CHAPTER 1

The Importance of Peer Competence and Social Inclusion

ICHAEL IS 4 YEARS OLD. He has been in preschool for 3 months, and is not well liked by his classmates. His favorite center is the block area. Michael often tries to enter into block play after a group of children have been playing there for 5 minutes or so. He typically storms into the area, announcing play intentions that are radically different from those of the group already engaged in play. "This is a racetrack!" he shouts. "We're making a space station," retorts Brian, with a defensive edge in his voice. Michael begins to run circles around the block area and in doing so, knocks over the space station. He grabs a block, crying out, "Here's the racetrack!" Brian clenches his fists and grimaces in frustration, while Ben lunges at Michael, saying in an angry voice, "You pig, Michael!"

Sarah, who is 6 years old, has recently begun kindergarten in a class with 17 typically developing peers. Sarah has developmental delay with mental retardation and autism. During the 30-minute free choice time, Sarah flits rapidly from one center to another. She may spend only a couple of seconds in a center, just long enough to grab a toy or other material and carry it to the next center to deposit it. Sometimes she stays in the housekeeping center for as long as one minute, touching, picking up, and rearranging the dress-up clothes, dishes, and dolls. Her activity appears to involve no pretending, and consists of simple manipulation of objects. As

1

she enters each center, she seems oblivious to the presence of other children. Her classmates generally ignore Sarah. A few actively avoid her, making comments like, "She's weird" or "She's just a baby."

Seven-year-old Maria is in first grade. In the lunchroom, she eats at the end of the table by herself, with her shoulders slumped and eyes downcast. On the playground, she longs to join the other girls as they play in the sand under the oak tree. She knows she could walk over and say, "Can I play with you?" She has some good ideas for fun things to play and talk about, but she envisions her attempts being rebuffed or ignored. Instead of taking a chance at "sounding stupid" or not being heard, she hangs back on the sidelines and busies herself playing with acorns. Only occasionally does she glance furtively at the activities of the other girls.

Each of the children in the examples above is experiencing difficulty in their interactions with peers. Michael appears not to use appropriate strategies for gaining access to play with peers, and seems to be developing a reputation as someone with whom interaction is unpleasant. Sarah seems to lack play skills, and does not appear to be interested in playing with her classmates. She is beginning to develop a reputation as a baby, as a child not to be included in classroom play. Maria may possess an awareness of socially competent strategies, but her fear and lack of self-confidence inhibit her ability to use what she knows. As time goes by, she may become increasingly invisible to her classmates.

In each of these examples, there is room for teachers to intervene for the purpose of promoting social competence with peers. The target of the teacher's support may be the individual child who is experiencing difficulty, members of the peer group who are not accepting that child, or both. In each of these examples, a child's well-being and happiness are at stake.

SOCIAL COMPETENCE AND PEER COMPETENCE

What exactly is meant by the term *social competence*? It seems that the number of definitions of social competence is nearly equal to the number of researchers interested in the topic! Some have suggested that how well children perceive, interpret, and respond to the variety of social situations they meet is a measure of their social competence (Kostelnik, Stein, Whiren, & Soderman, 1998). According to Katz and McClellan (1997), "Socially competent young children are those who engage in satisfying interactions and activities with adults and peers and through such interactions further their own competence" (p. 1). Social competence has also been described as the "ability to achieve personal goals in social interaction while simultaneously maintaining positive relationships with others over time and across situations" (Rubin & Rose-Krasnor, 1992, p. 285). This definition highlights the importance of balancing personal desires against social consequences, and places the needs and wants of the individual within social context.

In North American society, a high level of social competence generally means that a person exhibits responsible, independent, friendly, cooperative, purposeful, and self-controlled behavior. Those children who, by contrast, act irresponsibly, timidly, hostilely, uncooperatively, or impulsively are considered less socially competent (Knopczyk & Rodes, 1996). Other behaviors associated with social competence include giving and receiving emotional support, possessing social awareness, processing information accurately, communicating, problem-solving, and self-monitoring (Goleman, 1995). During the toddler years, social skills include:

- Coordinating behavior with that of a play partner
- Imitation of a peer's activity and an awareness of being imitated
- Turn taking that involves sequences of observe peer/respond to peer/ observe and wait/respond to peer
- Helping and sharing behaviors
- Responding appropriately to the peer partner's characteristics

During the preschool years, socially skilled behaviors are also marked by the ability to:

- Share meaning through social pretend play and rough-and-tumble play
- Use speech forms that demonstrate an understanding of the listener's characteristics
- Spontaneously direct prosocial behaviors to peers
(Rubin, Bukowski, & Parker, 1998)

Although consensus as to the full meaning of the term *social competence* remains elusive, Guralnick and Neville (1997) point out that there is general agreement among definitions that social competence refers to how an individual defines and solves the most fundamental challenges in human relationships. These fundamental challenges include the ability to initiate and sustain interactions with others, to resolve conflicts, to build friendships, and to achieve related interpersonal goals.

Peer competence, then, is competence in interactions with peers. A peer can be defined as an individual of roughly the same age and developmental level. Thus, peer competence refers to how a child defines and solves the fundamental challenges of initiating and sustaining interactions with peers, resolving conflicts with peers, and building friendships with peers. Furthermore, most definitions include elements of a child's effectiveness in influencing a peer's social behavior and appropriateness given a specific setting, context, and/or culture. Socially incompetent behavior could be characterized by social ineffectiveness (the lack of a positive effect on a peer's behavior or absence of any peer-directed behavior) or inappropriate use of social behaviors, given a particular social context (Guralnick, 1993). In the example describing Michael's behavior in the block center, Michael demonstrates difficulty in resolving a conflict of intentions. His behavior (storming in and announcing that "this is the racetrack") is inappropriate given a social context in which children are already engaged in creating a space station. Sarah exhibits an absence of any peer-directed behavior. Maria is ineffective in influencing her peers' behavior because she is anxious and inhibited with regard to attempting initiation strategies and friendship-building behaviors.

WHY IS COMPETENT PEER INTERACTION IMPORTANT?

As more parents of young children join the workforce, greater numbers of young children are placed in group care settings. Children in modern society experience social interaction with peers at a younger age and for longer periods of time. This increased exposure to peers has heightened interest in the significance of peer relationships for children's development. The research literature suggests that peer relationships contribute to children's long-term development in unique and important ways. The ability to interact effectively with peers is viewed as an important component of school readiness and is predictive of children's positive adjustment to school (Birch & Ladd, 1996; National Association for the Education of Young Children [NAEYC], 1995).

Peer relationships provide children with opportunities to interact with relative equals. Because of this equality, peer interactions present children with different challenges and different opportunities to play a variety of roles than do interactions with adults. The peer group is a special context in which children learn and practice the give and take that is important for competent social interaction (Hartup & Moore, 1991). For example, when resolving a conflict with an adult or older child, the conflict is likely to be resolved as a result of the older party's greater social skill or status. Being older and wiser, adults can control interactions with children. These hierarchical relationships are largely defined by control and compliance. Resolving a conflict with an age-mate, however, makes important growth-inducing demands upon the perspective-taking and communication skills of the children involved.

Consider, for example, a pair of 3-year-olds engaged in playing house. When Veronica plays "mommy," she is really playing "Veronica's mommy" and playing house means playing at the way things are in Veronica's house. So, too, for her play partner Lakeesha. When Lakeesha announces that it is time for the mommy to mow the lawn, Veronica is dumbstruck. That is impossible, only Dad mows the lawn. The argument that ensues is a growth experience for both girls. For Veronica, learning from a peer that mothers can cut the grass is a meaningful form of learning. Had an adult informed Veronica of this fact, she may have accepted it as fact, without examining it (simply because the teacher is a grown-up) and therefore without really processing it.

Peers present a rich source of cognitive conflict; cognitive conflict creates a sense of disequilibrium in children, which pushes them to try to fit new information with their existing understanding. Peers lead children to reflect on their own thinking and to adapt to the perspectives of others (Tudge & Caruso, 1988). In interaction with adults, children gain much information as "matters of fact." Knowledge induced by confrontations with adults largely results in changes in the child's thinking via compliance or conformity with the adult's point of view. Interactions with peers, by contrast, offer children a chance to negotiate, and thereby produce knowledge via consensus rather than via compliance (Hartup & Moore, 1991).

In the field of early childhood education (ECE), children's ability to engage in social play with peers has traditionally been accorded a significant role, one that has been strongly supported by prominent position papers (Bredekamp & Copple, 1997; NAEYC and National Association of Early Childhood Specialists in State Departments of Education [NAECS/SDE], 1991; Odom & McLean, 1996). Social competence serves as an important means for promoting independence, a long-established priority associated with developmentally appropriate practice. Outcome studies of the effect of early childhood education have revealed social variables to be among the most robust outcomes (Lazar, Darlington, Murray, Royce, & Snipper, 1982; Schweinhart et al., 1986). Social competence has traditionally been considered a "primary goal" of Head Start (National Head Start Association, 1990, p. 2). Similarly, leaders in the field of early childhood special education (ECSE) proposed that the development of social competence be considered a central mission of programs serving young children with disabilities (Guralnick, 1990).

In lower-quality early childhood programs, in which peer experience may be less appropriately facilitated by teachers (Kemple, David, & Hysmith, 1997), early peer experience may have detrimental effects on children's development (Vandell & Corasaniti, 1990). Positive features of the social environment can facilitate overall adjustment (Birch & Ladd, 1996; DeWolfe & Benedict, 1997; Kontos & Wilcox-Herzog, 1997). The early childhood years are a powerful time for nurturing the development of positive peer relationships (Katz & McClellan, 1997). In a meta-analysis examining the results of a large number of studies of social skills training programs for young children, it appeared that interventions occurring during the preschool years had considerably greater effects than those occurring in middle or later childhood years (Schneider & Byrne, 1985).

"Children are not born knowing how to make friends and influence people" (Kostelnik, Soderman, & Whiren, 1999, p. 436). They do not come into the world knowing the rules of their particular society. Mastering the necessary skills for functioning effectively in society requires time, growth, and a variety of social experiences. In addition to nutrition and physical comfort, the need for human association is basic (Maslow, 1954). Until a child's essential needs, including positive association with others, have been met, they are limited in their ability to move beyond those realms into academic areas of learning. Time spent on providing opportunities, support, and instruction in the area of peer competence is not wasted time. It is not the icing on the cake, but rather an essential ingredient.

DEVELOPMENTALLY APPROPRIATE PRACTICE
AND SOCIAL COMPETENCE

Developmentally appropriate practice encompasses age-appropriateness, cultural appropriateness, and individual appropriateness (Bredekamp & Copple, 1997). When teachers make developmentally appropriate decisions about supporting children's emerging social competence, they draw upon what they know about the needs, interests, and abilities of an individual child, and what they know about the culture and social context within which children live (Kostelnik, Whiren, Soderman, Stein, & Gregory, 2002).

Age Appropriateness

Chronological age can serve as an indicator of children's capabilities and interests. Child development progresses in a relatively orderly and predictable sequence, but the rate at which young children develop particular competencies can vary from individual to individual. Children of the same age may vary widely in the development of social concepts and skills. For example, during the early childhood years children's conceptions of themselves and of others progress from a focus on concrete observable attributes and behaviors toward defining themselves and others in terms of internal personal traits and competencies. In the kindergarten and primary years, children's cognitive development progresses in ways that make them more capable of engaging in social comparison. In the primary grades, children become aware of and concerned with peer acceptance and popularity (Bredekamp & Copple, 1997).

During the preschool years, children's developing communicative, language, symbolic, and perspective-taking abilities enable greater engagement in cooperative play, including cooperative social pretend play. Sociodramatic play becomes an important context for peer interaction for preschool and kindergarten children. In the primary grades, children continue to engage with one another through pretend play, and also become more capable of and interested in participating in cooperative games with rules (Bredekamp & Copple, 1997).

Cultural Appropriateness

Research on cultural differences in expectations for social competence is limited (Rubin, Bukowski, & Parker, 1998). Social behaviors can carry different meanings in different social groups and cultures. For example, in some cultural groups it is considered a sign of disrespect if a child looks into the eyes of an adult while being reprimanded. In other culture groups, the situation is quite different: lack of eye contact in such a situation is interpreted as disrespect. Lack of awareness of such differences in social meaning can lead to significant misunderstanding. Freedom to express emotions is also influenced by culture. In some cultures, children are encouraged to fully experience and express their strongest feelings. Yet other cultures value containment of emotion.

The value placed on dependence and independence often varies with culture. In some cultures, interdependence among individuals is highly valued. Children may be encouraged to remain dependent upon adults for longer periods than in other cultures. It may be considered typical and desirable, for example, for a 3-year-old to be spoon-fed by an adult in a cultural context that values interdependence over independence. In this case, spoon-feeding may be seen as the means to the goal of assuring that the child is fed efficiently, and adult and child cooperate in the work of making that happen. In a culture in which independence weighs more heavily in the balance, encouraging the child's self-help skills (in this case, self-feeding) may be seen as having greater value.

Individual Appropriateness

While the concept of age-appropriateness helps us to be mindful of general sequences and typical age ranges in attainment of developmental landmarks, these do vary by individual. Although the concept of cultural appropriateness alerts us to possible differences in meaning, purpose, and value tied to social behaviors, wide differences may exist between subgroups within a culture and from family to family. Ultimately, the individual child must become the point of focus. Individual children differ in their biological predispositions; their history of experiences; and their interests, needs, and challenges. Their rates of development and individual developmental trajectory may vary, particularly for children with disabilities.

The frameworks of reflective teaching and professional collaboration (including collaboration with families) are offered in Chapter 2 as useful tools for assessing and meeting the needs of the individual child, informed in part by development and culture.

INCLUSION AND PEER COMPETENCE

At the same time that there has been a general increase in numbers of children in early childhood programs, there has also been an increase in the numbers of children with disabilities who are eligible for early childhood services. Public Law 99-457, the 1986 amendment to the Education of the Handicapped Act, extended the provision of early intervention programs to children with developmental delays and disabilities from birth to age 5. Federal legislation requires that children be educated in the "least restrictive environment." This means that, to the maximum extent possible, the classroom setting in which children with special needs are educated should be the same setting as that in which typically developing children are educated (Thomas & Russo, 1995). Data indicate that over 50% of all preschool children with disabilities who are receiving services are in some form of inclusive setting (United States Department of Education [USDOE], 1990).

Multiple definitions of inclusion exist. The common factor across definitions is that children with disabilities and children without disabilities are placed in the same setting, most often a classroom (Odom & Diamond, 1998). Successful inclusion can be further described as the "theoretical, social and curricular means for assuring that all children are fully accepted members of the learning communities in which they participate" (Mallory, 1994, p. 58). Inclusive schools strive to create an environment wherein the needs of all students are accommodated and success is fostered for each child, by integrating children with disabilities in the mainstream of regular education and providing them with the specialized services they need within the regular education program. Segregated services for children with disabilities serve to further isolate those children from their peers.

A strong and compelling argument for inclusion is the moral assertion that children with disabilities have the *right* to participate in activities of daily life and programs of education and recreation available to other children. All children have the right to a life that is as normal as possible: children with disabilities should experience the same (high-) quality early childhood programs as children without disabilities, should be helped to become fully participating members of the classroom community, and should be supported to develop positive relationships within that community (Odom & Diamond, 1998). Building upon the civil rights movement of the 1960s, the disability rights movement has cited the core social values of equal opportunity for all citizens and maximum feasible participation as founded in the inalienable right of all people, including those with disabilities, for meaningful involvement in all social institutions.

The developmental significance of competence in peer interaction is recognized by early interventionists concerned with children with disabilities (Odom, McConnell, & McEvoy, 1992). In early childhood education programs, the inclusion of young children with disabilities is perceived by many educators as particularly important, as it is often the first formal situation in which children establish peer relationships. Two purposes of inclusion are to provide opportunities for children with disabilities to develop social interaction skills through interactions with typically developing children, and to increase typically developing children's acceptance of and compassion for children with disabilities through close social interaction (Odom & Brown, 1993). Recent research has demonstrated that participation in an inclusive early childhood program can positively impact children's readiness to accept peers with disabilities (Diamond, Hestenes, Carpenter, & Innes, 1997). Furthermore, children with positive attitudes toward peers with disabilities play more with peers with disabilities, as compared to children with less positive attitudes (Okagaki, Diamond, Kontos, & Hestenes, 1998). Successful peer interaction has been identified as an important contributor to self-efficacy of children with disabilities, and as a critical precursor to general community adjustment as an adult (Guralnick, 1990). The inclusive classroom arrangement provides the potential for children with disabilities to build friendships with typically developing peers, to benefit from the availability of appropriate peer models, and to use skills in a context that provides realistic social consequences (Guralnick, 1990; Odom & Brown, 1993).

Consider, for example, 4-year-old Frances, who is included in a community preschool program. Frances, whose communication development is delayed, has 15 typically developing peers in his classroom. His inclusion in this program affords him 15 potential friends, among whom he can find similar interests and compatibility. The special education class in which he was enrolled last year consisted of five children, and Frances did not develop a friendship during that year. His inclusion this year allows him to observe and imitate the normal communication behaviors of typical 4- and 5-year-olds, and to be reinforced by peers' elaborations in response to his communicative efforts. In his previous segregated class, three of Frances's peers were nonverbal, and he had few opportunities to learn from peer models or experience the reward of verbal peer responses. For a child with a disability in a segregated special education setting in which there are only peers who also have limited social interaction skills, opportunities for social skill acquisition may be lacking.

It has been well documented that a substantial proportion of young children with developmental disabilities experience significant problems in peer-related social competence (Odom, Zercher, Marquart, Li, Sandall, & Wolfberg, 2002). These difficulties are much greater than expected on the basis of children's level of cognitive development (Guralnick, 1990). Preschool–age children with developmental delays often engage in fewer social interactions and less mature social behavior than same-age peers without disabilities. Studies of mainstreaming have documented differences in the frequencies of social interaction of young children with disabilities (Guralnick, 1999). The lesser amount of peer interaction observed in children with disabilities may be due to less competence in engaging peers in interaction, may be due to rejection by peers, or may be due to the greater amount of time children with disabilities spend (in comparison to children without disabilities) in interactions with adults. Although not all young children with disabilities display difficulties in peer-related social competence, preschool special education teachers have reported that, on the average, 75% of the children in their classrooms need to learn to interact with their peers in a more positive and age-appropriate manner (Odom, McConnell, & Chandler, 1993).

A number of studies have shown that peer interaction for children with disabilities occurs more frequently in inclusive settings than in non-inclusive settings containing only children with disabilities (Odom & Diamond, 1998). Unfortunately, however, empirical evidence suggests that when children with disabilities are *merely physically placed* into regular early childhood programs, they have limited contact with normally developing peers. Children without disabilities tend to prefer interaction with other typically developing children (Guralnick, 1999; Guralnick, Gottman, & Hammond, 1996). Social rejection by peers is more common for children with disabilities than for typically developing children (Guralnick & Neville, 1997). Lack of successful social integration threatens the achievement of educational and socioemotional goals that are predicated upon children's participation in the peer group. True social inclusion requires intentional facilitation by skilled and knowledgeable adults.

Young children who do not possess the necessary social skills to enter or maintain satisfying interactions with peers are caught in a conundrum. They lack the skills for engaging in social interaction, yet participation in peer social interaction is the primary avenue through which they will learn more advanced forms of social competence. For some children with disabilities (as well as for some children without disabilities), nonsocial variables, such as unusual physical appearance, may exacerbate the situation and further prevent the child from establishing friendships in the classroom (Hymel, Wagner, & Butler, 1990). The classroom teacher is in a position to help children gain access to the arena of peer interaction, and to facilitate the acquisition of social skills within that context.

THE TEACHER'S ROLE

Why Do Teachers Have a Role?

The early childhood teacher plays a very important role in facilitating the development of young children's peer competence, partly by virtue of the fact that teachers are the adults who oversee children in peer group settings. While children's developing social competence with peers is certainly very substantially affected by the family and the larger community, the classroom teacher is the adult who knows and observes children most intimately within the peer group setting. The teacher is positioned to teach and provide support. Consider the following examples (Kemple & Hartle, 1999):

> It is Friday afternoon, and Mr. Casey is preparing his kindergarten classroom for the following week. He equips the block area with construction hats, rubber tools, and construction vehicles. He makes a note to himself to read *Mike Mulligan and his Steam Shovel* (Lee, 1939) at story time on Monday, and to provide books related to building construction in the literature corner. He has planned a short field trip to observe a nearby construction site on Tuesday. Mr. Casey has found that certain children in his class, like Terrance, are more successful in interacting with peers in the block area when a theme is suggested and supported by props, literature, and some common experience.
>
> Mrs. Talbot's second grade class will be gaining a new member next week. The new child, Carson, has multiple disabilities and uses a wheelchair.

The girl's parents have expressed concern that she will have difficulty making friends in her new classroom. Mrs. Talbot has already consulted with the special education liaison teacher about ways to help Carson become socially integrated into her new peer group. A willing and sociable child, Janine, will be Carson's "host" for the first week of school, helping her to "learn the ropes." Carson has been appointed "snack assistant," which means she will pass out placemats bearing classmates' names. This will allow her a special opportunity to interact with peers and learn their names. (p. 139)

Mr. Casey and Mrs. Talbot have several things in common. They are early childhood teachers who recognize the importance of young children's peer relationships. They hold the development of peer competence as an important goal for the children in their classrooms. They believe that they, as teachers, can have a positive influence on children's peer interactions, and they act planfully and intentionally to promote peer competence in their classrooms.

In many cases, positive and satisfying peer relationships do not magically occur simply because young children are in close and frequent proximity in a classroom or on a playground. The development of social competence in the peer group setting requires the attention of an adult who understands the social needs and capabilities of young children and who knows how to provide appropriate support and intervention when needed. Quality programs, teachers well versed in inclusive practices, and innovative curricula can help to promote the development of social competence, and can foster social inclusion.

What Is the Nature of Teachers' Roles?

Ramsey (1991) has identified three complementary approaches to promoting peer relationships in early childhood classrooms. General teaching practices and the overall organization and structure of the classroom constitute a macro-level influence on the quality of children's peer interactions. These may influence the quality of children's peer interactions by affecting the emotional climate and opportunities for peer interaction (Kontos & Wilcox-Herzog, 1997). For example, routines and schedules may affect the social dynamics of a classroom by conveying teachers' social priorities and through the degree of freedom and time they allow for children to interact in an informal manner.

A second means by which teachers may attempt to promote children peer relationships is their use of curriculum materials and activities that support social skills and peer relationships. For example, teachers may use cooperative games, social problem-solving exercises, role-playing activities, and stories in their efforts to develop children's understanding of social responsibility, the nature of social relationships, and how to be a "good friend."

Finally, teachers may influence children's peer competence through planned or spontaneous social interventions, implemented by either the teacher or another designated adult, either within or outside the classroom environment. Such intervention strategies include modeling, coaching, peer pairing, social problem-solving methods, and methods combining these approaches.

Teachers have a multitude of opportunities to support children's developing social competence in a variety of ways. When teachers arrange aspects of the classroom environment and provide materials and props to encourage social interaction and social play, schedule sufficient free play, establish routines that allow children to be as independent and competent as they can be, and institute a positive system of management and discipline, they help to support children's peer relationships. When these basic supports are in place, teachers have set the stage for using on-the-spot facilitation of children's naturally occurring interactions, planned activities that support and encourage peer interaction and the appropriate use of social skills, as well as more structured, adult-directed social skills training efforts. The support of a high-quality program, well-honed skills of observation and assessment, a sound understanding of developmentally appropriate practice, and knowledge of inclusive practices are important foundations for the teacher who values and strives to nurture the growth of all young children's social competence with peers.

SUMMARY

Interest in the importance of young children's peer relationships and peer competence has grown, as more children spend greater time with peers at younger ages. Positive peer relationships appear to be important to children's development and adjustment. The peer group is a unique and significant context for the growth of social skills for all children. For young children with disabilities, the opportunity to interact with, learn from, and develop friendships with typically developing peers is a central purpose of inclusion. Unfortunately, peer competence and friendships often do not spontaneously emerge when children are simply placed in a setting with peers. Teachers play essential roles as they set the stage for children's interactions and intervene to support children's developing social interaction skills. Teachers who value peer competence, who recognize the centrality

of their role in promoting competent peer interaction, and who act thoughtfully and intentionally to support peer competence can make a substantial
contribution to this important area of children's development.

FOOD FOR THOUGHT

1. Think about a young child you know, whom you consider to be socially
   competent. What are some of the behaviors and characteristics that
   seem to contribute to that child's social competence? Think about another young child you know, whom you consider to be less socially
   competent. What are some of the behaviors and characteristics that contribute to that child's social difficulties. Can you think of some skills or
   understandings that child might develop that would enhance his or her
   social competence?

2. Reread the scenario at the beginning of this chapter describing Maria's
   behavior. Brainstorm a list of possible ways a teacher might be able to
   intervene with Maria, to help her make friends. Are there ways a teacher
   could intervene with Maria's *peers*, to help Maria gain acceptance to
   the peer group? What might those intervention strategies look like?

CHAPTER 2

Reflective Teaching and Collaboration as Unifying Frameworks for Social Inclusion

MANY EARLY CHILDHOOD PROGRAMS today include both young children with disabilities and typically developing peers. When children with disabilities are fully included in a regular classroom, professionals work together to ensure that the children's special needs are met within that "normalized" context. The classroom teacher can adapt his or her teaching strategies to best support each child, including a child with a disability. In addition, classroom assistants may be taught to work with an individual child, or to support the teacher's work with an individual child. Specialists in early childhood special education may serve as consultants to the classroom teacher, and may also provide direct services to a child within the regular classroom. Thus, professionals must work closely to meet the needs of all children in the classroom. Collaboration requires that professionals in early childhood education and early childhood special education share knowledge and understanding of the philosophies and approaches of both fields.

EARLY CHILDHOOD EDUCATION AND
EARLY CHILDHOOD SPECIAL EDUCATION

As inclusive early childhood education programs become more common, teachers are faced with the challenge of expanding their repertoire of teaching and guidance practices to accommodate the needs of all children. The success of an inclusive early education program rests on the ability of educators who are trained to meet the needs of children with a wide range of abilities and needs. Many early childhood teachers have limited training in early childhood special education and have not been extensively educated in methods for working with children with special needs. Many early childhood special educators are not well versed in the methods and philosophies of "general" early childhood education (Wolery & Bredekamp, 1994). When young children with and without disabilities are cared for and educated in the same programs, it is important that all teachers have understanding of and respect for the philosophy, research base, and practices of both disciplines. For example, to promote peer skills, general early childhood educators have traditionally relied most heavily on naturalistic teaching (to be described in Chapter 4), while early childhood special educators have more commonly utilized more direct, high-intensity behavioral interventions, tailored to individual children (to be described in Chapter 6) (Conroy, Langenbrunner, & Burleson, 1996; Wolery & Bredekamp, 1994). Recently, more naturalistic approaches have gained visibility in the ECSE (Early Childhood Special Education) literature (e.g., Brown & Odom, 1995; Brown, Odom, & Conroy, 2001). As children with and without disabilities are educated together, it behooves teachers to possess a wide variety of strategies in their repertoire; teachers can then choose interventions based on situational and individual needs.

The fields of early childhood education and early childhood special education have much in common. Obviously, both are concerned with promoting the education and welfare of young children. Both have traditionally emphasized the importance of family involvement, and both have emphasized the importance of attending to individual differences (Bredekamp, 1993).

Historically, differences have existed between early childhood special and general education teachers, including different educational preparation, separate professional organizations, and reliance on different bodies of research (Wolery & Wilbers, 1994). The theoretical foundations of the two disciplines have some commonalities and differences. Both ECE and ECSE practices are based in constructivist perspectives (e.g., Piaget, 1963; Vygotsky, 1978). ECE, however, also has historical roots in the maturational perspective, while ECSE has historical roots in the behavioral tradition (Wolery & Bredekamp, 1994). The assumptions of maturational and behavioral perspectives are different, so it is not surprising that some differences in practices would emerge. The maturational perspective (which emphasizes the natural unfolding of development according to an inborn timetable) suggests a "let's wait and see, he'll probably grow out of it" approach. The behavioral perspective (which focuses on external antecedents and consequences of behavior) suggests intervention.

> Early childhood educators too often err on the side of withholding involvement and may miss opportunities to challenge and support children's learning; on the other hand, early childhood special educators are so well trained to intervene that they may err on the side of intervening when less directive strategies such as supporting play and peer interaction may also be effective. (Bredekamp, 1993, p. 267)

This theoretical distinction, of course, represents a simplification. Within each field there probably exists as much variation as exists between the two fields. Not all ECE professionals share the same beliefs and practices, just as ECSE professionals differ among themselves in their beliefs and preferred methods. Both fields are somewhat eclectic and are diversely populated by individuals with their own belief systems. More important, the trend has been toward a merging of theoretical bases. A "convergent" theoretical model, which identifies and builds upon the commonalities across the three theoretical traditions, has been advocated as a more useful foundation for inclusive practices (Mallory, 1994).

The two disciplines of ECE and ECSE have traditionally served different populations of children. Much of the research in ECE has been driven by the need to support young typically developing children who are at risk for developmental problems. ECSE research, on the other hand, has been focused on intervening to address developmental problems for children with disabilities. Intervention has been the hallmark of ECSE, while ECE has been characterized as enrichment (Wolery & Bredekamp, 1994). A critical premise of programs for young children with disabilities is that practices must be outcome-based (Carta, Schwartz, Atwater, & McConnell, 1991). The goal of intervention is to intervene to move the child toward a desired outcome or goal that he or she would not likely achieve without intervention. ECE has traditionally not placed as much emphasis on outcomes as ECSE has and must (Wolery & Bredekamp, 1994).

Individualization has traditionally been a hallmark of both ECE and ECSE, but has been practiced somewhat differently in the two fields. In ECE, greater attention has been accorded to individual interests. This has been evident, for instance, in the wide array of activity choices made available to children in a quality early childhood program. In ECSE, greater attention has been accorded to individual abilities and needs, and planning teaching strategies that are in line with a child's abilities, and are directed toward meeting his or her needs. ECE has been less systematic in ensuring that individual children's needs are met in relation to program goals, and has focused more on providing experiences that are age-appropriate and less on meeting individual developmental variation.

Each field has a rich tradition of literature on the topic of promoting social competence. Some of this literature consists of research, which provides empirical validation for specifically described intervention methods. Some provides suggestions for strategies derived from principles of child development and learning that have been empirically supported by research. Other suggestions for promoting social competence have been derived from the practical wisdom of teachers, developed through many years of first-hand experience working with young children. It is a basic premise of this book that all of these sources of information are of value and potential use to teachers who strive to support young children in their developing ability to interact effectively and appropriately with peers.

CONTINUUM OF STRATEGIES

In 1987, NAEYC published *Developmentally Appropriate Practice in Early Childhood Programs Serving Children from Birth to Age Eight* (Bredekamp, 1987), which was revised and published in 1997 as *Developmentally Appropriate Practices in Early Childhood Programs* (Bredekamp & Copple, 1997). Many have argued that developmentally appropriate practice (DAP) provides an appropriate educational context for the inclusion of young children with disabilities, when interpretations of DAP guidelines leave room for adaptations and extensions to meet the child's specific needs (Carta, 1995; Wolery & Bredekamp, 1994; Wolery, Werts, & Holcombe-Ligon, 1994). For some young children, this may mean the use of behavioral strategies such as planned programs of systematic reinforcement. If inclusion is to succeed, it is necessary for teachers to be open to the possibility of using such strategies for particular children in particular circumstances. Developmentally appropriate practice must, by definition, be individually appropriate.

It is important to tailor teaching approaches to be congruent with the identified goals for the child(ren), the demands of a particular situation, and the competencies of the child or children involved. Adjusting teaching to be individually appropriate implies that effective facilitation strategies fall along a continuum of directiveness, from least teacher-controlled to most teacher-controlled. This continuum of directiveness can be considered from the perspective of Vygotskian theory (File, 1993). The application of Vygotskian principles to the realm of peer interaction suggests that children can interact more effectively when they receive the individually appropriate level of adult support. Some children, in some situations, may require no adult intervention at all; they may be able to function in a socially competent manner when simply provided with toys, time, and access to peers. Some may be able to function competently when an adult maintains an attentive presence in the situation but does not offer help. Some may need an adult to identify important social cues or to verbally interpret social behavior. Some may require demonstration, in which the adult shows a child, during the course of natural interaction, an example of a strategy to use. Some children may need intensive instruction and practice in social skills outside of the natural setting, accompanied by explicit prompts to use newly learned skills in natural settings. Some children may need systematic social and tangible reinforcement for engaging in interaction and/or for using newly acquired skills with peers.

The teacher's continuing challenge is to decide which approach to use for which children, depending upon the competencies to be developed and the nature of the immediate situation. To meet the challenge, a teacher must be a keen, sensitive, informed observer of children's behavior, and must also have at his or her disposal a wide range of intervention options from which to choose. As a general rule, teachers may begin by considering the least intrusive and most "normalized" interventions (those requiring the minimum change in classroom routine and the minimum amount of additional resources). If that level of intervention is deemed to be inadequate, the teacher moves up to consider interventions of a higher intensity (Brown & Conroy, 1997; Brown, Odom, & Conroy, 2001; Odom & Brown, 1993). It has also been suggested that teachers employ classwide interventions (inclusion, provision of a general developmentally appropriate program) first, and then employ individualized interventions as necessary (Brown & Conroy, 1997). As the field of early childhood special education has expanded its theoretical base to incorporate a developmental framework, interest has expanded in interventions embedded in the ongoing routines and activities of classroom life (see Bricker, 1989; Guralnick, 1993). There is growing agreement among professionals in early childhood special education and early childhood education that naturalistic strategies be tried before considering more teacher-directed approaches such as social skills training groups and direct teacher reinforcement of desired social behaviors (Conroy, Langenbrunner, & Burleson, 1996).

The combined traditions of ECE and ECSE offer a wide range of strategies for encouraging, supporting, and intervening in children's peer relationships and developing peer skills. As previously described, the strategies suggested by ECE have tended to focus on "setting the stage" by providing time, materials, and a supportive environment as context for promoting peer interaction. The strategies of early childhood special educators have tended to be more highly structured, intensive training interventions. In recent years, however, ECSE researchers have advocated for trying more naturalistic interventions first. In ECE, there are examples of more structured approaches as well (e.g., McGinnis & Goldstein, 1990; Mize, Ladd, & Price, 1985; Shure, 1992). As inclusion pulls the two fields into closer collaboration, the options considered should broaden. The philosophical framework of reflective teaching can provide a helpful perspective to the professional faced with a potentially overwhelming range of support and intervention options. Reflection is an essential ingredient to making good choices from within the combined methods and strategies of ECE and ECSE.

REFLECTIVE TEACHING

Reflective teachers are those who view teaching as a continual problem-solving process. Reflective teachers do not approach teaching as a "follow the recipe" enterprise and do not adhere rigidly to a prescribed and limited set of practices. Reflective teachers are knowledgeable and informed professionals who are empowered to make reasoned, deliberate, and ethical choices about important goals for the children they teach, and about appropriate strategies to meet those goals. Reflective teachers assess the results of the teaching methods they employ and assume responsibility for their decisions. The process of reflective teaching does not mandate the decisions teachers will make but rather ensures that those decisions will be constantly reevaluated with regard to their actual observed impact.

An important assumption of reflective teaching is that there are no fixed answers to the problems of learning and teaching. Teaching is difficult, complex, and constantly requires that teachers use their judgment. Discussing the challenges of teaching, Ross, Bondy, and Kyle (1993) suggest

> Many times . . . you will wish someone would tell you what to do and how to do it. We wish we had the answers, but we don't. No one does, and teach-

ers should be very wary of those who claim they do, because such people lack an understanding of the basic nature of teaching. (p. 11)

Another related assumption of reflective teaching is that research does not have all the answers. In this book, you will encounter a variety of intervention and support strategies whose effectiveness has been supported by research. You will also encounter many potentially powerful and useful strategies that have been indirectly supported by research, or for which conclusive research is very difficult or impossible to carry out, or for which the research has simply not yet been conducted. Research is useful because it provides information: it can provide information about strategies that have worked for a particular child (or sample population of children) for a particular purpose, and under a particular set of circumstances. No matter how much research is carried out, however, research will never provide teachers with definitive *answers*. Research cannot dictate a set of teaching strategies that will be guaranteed effective for all (or any) children. Ultimately, it falls to the classroom professional (or a group of professionals working in collaboration) to select strategies that seem most likely to apply to the characteristics of the child or children with whom they are to be used, the goals that have been identified for that child or children, and the details of the particular classroom context.

A third assumption of the reflective teaching framework is that teaching requires a commitment to professional development and growth. This implies an openness to new ideas, and a willingness to make the time and do the mental work necessary for professional enhancement. In this book, you will probably encounter some strategies that are new to you. You will probably encounter some strategies that do not immediately resonate with your own belief system, that seem foreign or strange or even wrong. I will encourage you to examine why you react in this way, and to consider particular situations and children for which an approach that at first glance seems odd, intrusive, overly simple, or too complicated might actually be an appropriate choice.

The process of reflective teaching can be depicted with the diagram in Figure 2.1. The reflective teaching cycle begins with an *experienced dilemma* (Dewey, 1933). A dilemma is a problematic situation for which no readily identifiable solution is apparent. For example, Ms. Smith notices that 3-year-old Carrie is often rejected when she requests of other children, "Can I play with you?" After the teacher has identified a dilemma to be addressed, he or she *plans* by (1) defining the problem and (2) actively searching for a desirable solution. Problem definition is very important, because some definitions will restrict the range of alternatives the teacher considers, and may thereby prevent successful solution of the dilemma. For

Figure 2.1. The Cycle of Reflective Teaching

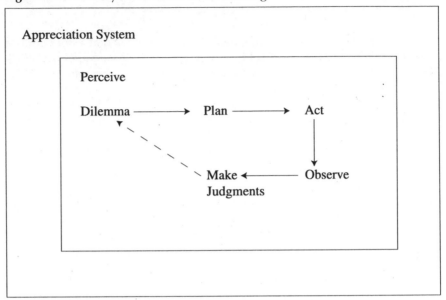

Adapted from Ross, Bondy, and Kyle (1993).

example, if Ms. Smith defines the problem as "How can I convince the other children that they must let Carrie play?" she will most likely focus on solutions that are targeted toward the other children, and that consist of motivating, reasoning with, and/or rewarding them for allowing Carrie to join their play. If, on the other hand, Ms. Smith defines the problem as "How can I help Carrie learn more effective play entry strategies?" she will be likely to consider solutions that target Carrie's behavior, such as coaching, modeling entry behaviors, and prompting.

The dilemma initially perceived by Ms. Smith could be defined in a variety of ways. The nature and number of dilemmas that a teacher perceives, and the way he or she defines the problem, are strongly influenced by the teacher's appreciation system, or specialized knowledge (Schon, 1983).

An appreciation system includes a teacher's:

- Beliefs about teaching, learning, children, and the purpose of schooling
- Knowledge of relevant theory and research
- Experiences with children
- Knowledge of the competencies to be taught

- Knowledge of the purpose and likely consequences of various teaching strategies
- Sensitivity to the child's point of view

(Ross, Bondy, & Kyle, 1993)

A teacher's storehouse of values, knowledge, theories, and practices influences his or her ability to perceive dilemmas, define problems, identify solutions, and assess the effect of attempted solutions.

After initially defining the problem, Ms. Smith searches for a desirable solution by going through the mental process of considering a variety of alternative solutions and considering the potential consequences of each. Working from the second problem definition, "How can I help Carrie develop more effective play entry strategies?", she thinks:

The problem could be that Carrie waits too long after play time begins, before she tries to become involved with a group. By that time, the play may be so well-established that Carrie's entry becomes more difficult than would be the case if she became involved with a group right at the start of free play time. But no, now that I think of it, I have observed that she often does try to join groups as they are forming, by asking, "Can I play, too?" and she is usually rejected. Come to think of it, the only bid for entry I've ever heard her use is "Can I play, too?" It seems that the other children have developed an almost automatic "no" response to this bid. Perhaps if she knew a couple of other more subtle entry strategies, she'd be more successful. Also, I may need to find a way to alter the other children's exclusionary responses, since it seems to have become a habit to say "no" to Carrie . . . I remember reading in my continuing education class that sometimes helping a child learn new social skills is not effective in helping that child gain acceptance, because the established perceptions of his or her peers might not readily change in response to the child's new skills. I could arrange to be close to Carrie as play time begins, and encourage her to find a role that she could contribute to the play theme that is forming. . . . I've heard other teachers say that strategy often works. To begin with, I may need to directly suggest a specific role, like, "You could be the cook. Here, stand at the stove and stir this soup." I could encourage the other children to see the value of Carrie's participation by suggesting ways they can interact with the role she has contributed, like, "Carrie has made a nice soup. Get your bowls!"

As you can see, in the process of considering possible solutions, Ms. Smith has simultaneously refined her definition of the problem. Ms. Smith's next step is to *act* by carrying out her plan, *observe* what occurs, and *make judgments* about the success or failure of the plan in light of her goals and ethical commitments. Ms. Smith begins to observe Carrie's behavior and the behavior of the other children as soon as she begins to implement her plan, and immediately begins the process of making judgments about both intended and possible unintended consequences of the plan.

In the first couple of days, she sees that Carrie is gaining entry to the play situation, and stays to play for an extended period. She considers whether her intervention may have the undesirable effect of directing and controlling the children's play, but observes that the children do not become "stuck" on her play suggestions. Instead, they transform and build upon the play theme, and continue to include Carrie as the play transforms from cooking soup, to preparing babies for an outing, to chasing witches from the house. Ms. Smith jots brief anecdotal records each day describing her intervention and the behaviors of Carrie and the other children involved.

After 2 weeks of this simple intervention, Ms. Smith has observed that Carrie is being included in play, but that Carrie seems to be dependent upon Ms. Smith to suggest her role and invite the other children to integrate that role. This presents a new dilemma. To address this unintended consequence, Ms. Smith decides to revamp her intervention to withdraw some of her direct support and give Carrie greater responsibility. Instead of making suggestions during the course of Carrie's entry to play, Ms. Smith makes a plan to very briefly coach Carrie in advance by reminding her of the variety of roles Carrie has played so far, and suggesting that Carrie choose one and try it out. Ms. Smith does not enter the play area herself, but stays within earshot in case her support is needed. Ms. Smith then completes the reflective process again by carrying out her plan, observing, and making judgments. By the end of the 3rd week, Carrie is frequently successful in entering the dramatic play area with only minimal advance coaching by Miss Smith.

The process of naturalistic observation is an important component of the reflective teaching cycle. Naturalistic observation is an invaluable means both of assessing children's peer skills and assessing the effectiveness of interventions to enhance social competence. A thorough discussion of methods of naturalistic observation is beyond the scope of this book. The following are good sources of information about collecting observational assessment data: Almy and Genishi (1979); Chandler and Dahlquist (2002); Cohen, Stern, and Balaban (1997); Neilsen, Olive, Donovan, and McEvoy (1999); Wolery (1994a); and Zirpoli (1995).

COLLABORATION AND REFLECTION

As it has been described so far, the cycle of reflection may appear to be primarily an internal, intra-individual process. It often is, as in the example of Ms. Smith's reflections and actions regarding Carrie's social needs. The reflective process can also be an interpersonal, collaborative enterprise. This social form of reflection may be of particular importance in inclusive settings, where several experts from a variety of realms (parents, the early childhood professional, the early childhood special education professional, the speech therapist, the school psychologist, and so forth) work together to make plans for meeting children's special needs.

As children with varying abilities and needs are cared for and educated together, it is imperative that the expertise of general early childhood education and early childhood special education be tapped to ensure the best outcomes for children. One avenue by which this can and should happen is by teachers broadening their range of knowledge to include the knowledge bases of both ECSE and general ECE. This can occur through the unified, transdisciplinary preparation of teachers of young children (Correa et al., 1997; Kemple, Hartle, Correa, & Fox, 1994; Lowenthal, 1992; Miller, 1992). To some extent, this can also occur through in-service education, conference workshops, and other professional development experiences. Another very important means by which the wealth of knowledge of allied disciplines are brought to bear on practice is through the establishment and nurturing of collaborative reflection and decision making among professionals concerned with meeting the needs of young children in early childhood settings.

Collaboration has been described as "more than a coming together. . . . At best, it requires that the participants reach a new level of understanding—a perspective that was not apparent before" (Jones & Nimmo, 1999, p. 6). Collaboration requires dialog. Dialog involves more than "simply talking to each other, swapping points of view and then leaving to make up *your* mind. It involves being prepared to wrestle with another's perspectives" (p. 7). Collaborative working relationships differ from simple coordination of effort. In coordinated efforts, the individuals or groups involved remain independent. In collaboration, decision-making is shared and solutions are the result of sharing perspectives and working to come to a consensus solution that is mutually satisfactory. In collaborative efforts, previously independent groups or individuals work together in a new organizational structure in order to achieve common goals that could not be effectively accomplished by either group independently (Kagan, 1991).

A *transdisciplinary* approach to assessing individual needs and making plans for intervention differs in important ways from methods that are generally referred to as *multidisciplinary* and *interdisciplinary* (Bergen, 1994). In a multidisciplinary approach, several professionals (for example, a school psychologist, a special education teacher, the general classroom teacher, a behavior specialist, a speech pathologist) may each conduct a separate evaluation of a child, using the procedures common to their particular field of expertise. These results are then typically reported to one individual who serves as a central link. Plans for intervention are generally made by one or two individuals, using the written results of the various evaluations. There is no group meeting, and parental involvement is minimal. In an interdisciplinary approach, the various professionals share (in a group meeting including parents) the results of their individual evaluations. Each professional typically makes his or her own recommendations for intervention, and professionals generally do not comment on one another's evaluations or suggestions (Bergen, 1994).

A transdisciplinary approach looks quite different. When implemented in ideal form, the parents give their own assessment of their child's needs and their own areas of concern. The team (professionals and parents) work as a whole to decide what the appropriate methods of assessment are. Intervention plans are made by the team as a whole, based on discussion of the combined results of assessments. One of the many advantages of a transdisciplinary approach is that it helps the group to understand the whole child and the contexts within which he or she lives, which potentially leads to more comprehensive, efficient, and effective intervention efforts. Another advantage is that, through the process of sharing decision making and information, individual team members can experience a widened perspective and enriched knowledge (Bergen, 1994).

In collaborative transdisciplinary service delivery teams, team members engage together in a problem-solving process in which each team member contributes his or her knowledge and skills equally (Vandercook & York, 1990). A challenge of this approach is the development of collaboration between and among a group of individuals for a sustained length of time, during which multiple services and professionals are required by the child (Bruder, 1994). Collaboration of this nature requires significant investment of time and energy. In a transdisciplinary teaming approach, the main purpose is to pool and integrate the expertise of team members in order to provide both more efficient and more comprehensive service to the child. In this approach, team members must systematically cross discipline boundaries as they create plans for an individual child's program. The child's program is implemented by one person or a few people, but with ongoing assistance provided by various team members (Bruder, 1994).

Collaborative consultation, an easier approach to implement, involves give and take of information between two or more people for the purpose of (1) resolving a need, issue, or problem, and (2) improving the individuals' understanding of these issues and their ability to respond effectively to similar dilemmas in the future (Gutkin & Curtis, 1982). Collaborative consultation is a *part* of the transdisciplinary "teaming" process. Consultation can be used to provide either direct services (e.g., the consultant directly provides instruction to the child) or indirect services (e.g. the consultant helps enable the teacher to implement a particular instructional strategy with the child) (Idol, 1993). Optimal collaborative consultation requires that participants in the consultation have good communication skills, collaborative problem-solving skills, and the abilities to be caring, respectful, open, and empathic (West & Cannon, 1988).

Collaborative relationships among early childhood teachers and other professionals are an important marker of successful inclusion programs (Kontos & File, 1993). Successful collaborations are facilitated by such factors as shared philosophy, good communication, administrative support, and willingness to release one's professional role by sharing expertise (Lieber et al., 1997).

Look back now at the cycle of reflective teaching depicted in Figure 2.1, and consider it as an interpersonal, collaborative process. A *dilemma* may be perceived by an individual teacher, brought to a collaborative team, and described to that team based on that individual teacher's perceptions. The process of clearly defining the problem may involve exchange of tentative interpretations by various team members. Before the dilemma is defined, observation by one or two other team members may be warranted. Through this process, definition of the problem is being supported and influenced not by one teacher's appreciation system, but by the *appreciation systems* of a collection of individuals united as a team. In the process of problem definition (and throughout the collaborative reflection process), it is likely that all individuals' appreciation systems will be extended or modified to some degree. Drawing on the various areas of expertise that make up the team's collective appreciation system, consensus about an initial *plan* of action is built. The plan may be *enacted* by just one member of the team (or more). *Observation* of the plan's outcomes (both intended and unintended) may be carried out by the same individual team member or others. Observations are brought back to the group for collaborative reflection targeted toward making *judgments* about the plan's effectiveness, judgments about whether a new plan is warranted, and judgments about whether new dilemmas have emerged that should be defined and addressed. All the while, the process is informed and supported by a "mega" appreciation system, which includes the pooled expertise and perspectives of variously trained and variously experienced team members.

SUMMARY

Both general and special early childhood educators recognize the importance of peer relationships and competence in peer interaction. Each discipline has a tradition of practical and research literature on the topic of promoting social competence. Though there has been some sharing and borrowing across the two disciplines, these two bodies of literature have developed somewhat independently. Now that children with and without disabilities are included in the same program, it is essential that teachers have familiarity with the broad continuum of approaches that have been offered by the two fields of early education. Awareness of and openness to a variety of approaches is one step toward enabling teachers to make good decisions about how to intervene with a particular child in a specific situation, in order to promote a desired outcome. Understanding and use of the process of reflective teaching can help teachers to identify needs, create and/or select interventions, enact those interventions, observe results, and make plans for further action. Understanding and use of collaborative strategies can help professionals to draw upon the collective wisdom, expertise, and experience of differently trained professionals as they create, carry out, and evaluate plans to support young children's developing peer competence.

FOOD FOR THOUGHT

1. Reread the scenario describing Michael's behavior in Chapter 1. Keeping in mind the cycle of reflection depicted in Figure 2.1, think about Michael's difficulty. What do you see as the dilemma in this scenario? What further information would you wish to have, in order to more fully define the problem in this situation? What plans might you formulate for the purpose of helping Michael and/or his peers?

    Now, discuss this dilemma with a small group of other adults who have also read and considered the scenario. As a team, engage in collaborative reflection regarding problem definition. What further information would your team wish to have in order to more fully define the problem? What plans might your team formulate for the purpose of helping Michael and/or his peers?

    How did the process of individual reflection differ from the collaborative reflection in which you engaged as a team? Was one process easier? Was one more difficult? Which was more fruitful? What are some potential benefits of individual reflection? Of collaborative reflection? What are some potential drawbacks of each? How could the drawbacks be minimized?

2. Reread the scenario describing Sarah's behavior in Chapter 1. Consider the continuum of strategies introduced in this chapter. What are some

less directive strategies that could be considered to help Sarah and/or her peers? What are some more structured strategies that could be considered? On what might your choice of strategies depend? What more would you wish to know about the children and the situation in order to make decisions about possible plans of action?

CHAPTER 3

Arranging the Environment to Support Peer Interaction

S OMETIMES THE MOST SUBTLE interventions to support peer interaction can be the most powerful. While their subtlety may be part of their potency, this may also result in their being overlooked, taken for granted, or left unexamined. In any early childhood education program, teachers and children interact within an environmental context. In this chapter, environmental context is viewed in a broad manner, as including the physical structures, objects, and organization of the room; the temporal organization of activities and routines; and the emotional climate of the setting. This embedded infrastructure sets the stage for what is possible.

The physical elements of every classroom are arranged in some way. Whether or not adults consciously recognize it, the physical attributes of the classroom setting (room arrangement, aesthetic qualities, materials provided) influence children's social interactions within that environment. The daily happenings of every class are in some way partitioned into time segments: there are particular times designated for engaging in different behaviors and activities. The degree of flexibility or rigidity of the schedule may vary dramatically from one classroom to another, as may the actual content and pacing of the schedule. Furthermore, every classroom differs in the degree and quality of acceptance, security, and community that is provided. A program that builds children's sense of predictability, feelings of genuine acceptance, and a climate of adult responsiveness attends to children's most basic emotional needs (Hyson, 1994). In the ecology of an emotionally rich and supportive community, children experience an essential foundation upon which social competence and healthy relationships are constructed.

In the sections that follow, readers are invited to consider ways that teachers can positively, intentionally, and reflectively create an environment to increase rates of positive interaction, support children's emerging peer interaction skills, and nurture the growth of satisfying relationships. The mere act of inclusion of children with varying abilities in a single program will be considered as a basic foundation for setting the stage to promote the peer competence of all children. Various elements of physical room arrangement, including location of furniture, organization of the classroom into separate areas and pathways, and aesthetic and sensory qualities of the environment, will be examined, as they are pertinent to promoting peer competence. Selection, organization, and accessibility of materials will be described, because these are related to children's likelihood of interaction, ability to share, and feelings of inclusion. Pacing, flexibility, and other elements of the daily schedule will be considered as part of the temporal environment, as will teachers' decisions about routines and transitions and the provision of time for daily activities with particular potential to encourage social development. The impact of the adult-child ratio, overall group size, and social density (number of children per square foot of space) will be discussed. Finally, ways of creating an accepting, secure, and supportive emotional climate within the classroom community will be considered. A positive emotional climate is emphasized as an essential, nonoptional foundation for supporting the development of peer interaction skills, the formation of friendships, and the realization of true social inclusion.

ROOM ARRANGEMENT

Sometimes it can be easier to change people's behavior indirectly, by altering the physical environment, than it is to modify their behavior directly. Those of us who are students or who teach adult students likely have noted that classroom interactions are different when students are seated in rows facing front as opposed to being in a large circle or being in small groups at tables. Different arrangements communicate different expectations for behavior and provide different degrees of support for comfortable interaction. Teachers' decisions about manipulation of physical attributes of the early childhood environment can have a potent effect on children's social interactions and emerging competence (Rogers-Warren, 1977). A number of research studies have demonstrated that the arrangement of physical space and provision of materials can affect children's behavior in the classroom. A carefully designed environment can decrease the occurrence of aggression and increase opportunities for such prosocial interactions as cooperating, sharing, and helping (Brown, Fox, & Brady, 1987; Sainato & Carta, 1992; Trawicke-Smith, 1990).

It is important to recognize that no recipe exists for creating the optimal physical environment. A teacher's skill and sensitivity as an observer are important tools in creating a classroom environment that works. The reflective cycle (Figure 2.1) is a useful representation to keep in mind as you identify environmental variables that may support or detract from the social quality of a particular classroom, plan and implement changes, assess the apparent results of those changes, and possibly create plans for new alterations. Two or three sets of eyes may be better than one in this process: pairs of teachers may share observations and collaborate to create potential solutions. Other observers (e.g., a psychologist, an architect, and even an interior designer) may be able to identify problems of physical arrangement that might be overlooked by the classroom teacher who spends many hours a day within the fours walls of her or his classroom.

Small-Group Interest Areas

Teachers can encourage social interaction by arranging the classroom into well-defined interest areas that accommodate small groups. The smaller clusters of children that result from such an arrangement may provide more manageable and inviting opportunities for peer play. Preschoolers generally tend to prefer interaction in small groups of two to four (Kostelnik et al., 2002). In kindergarten and the primary grades, children's growing social skills enable them to interact in somewhat larger groups.

There are a variety of strategies that teachers can use to create well-delineated interest areas. Furniture placement can create highly visible area boundaries, and a sense of privacy and protection for work and play. Think back for a moment to your own childhood. You may have memories of creating protected havens for play with siblings, or a small group of friends. A blanket thrown over a picnic table, a fort created with sofa cushions, a big box, or the seclusion of an attic space may have invited extended and complex (and therefore memorable) social play that may not otherwise have occurred. Research has documented that children generally do prefer enclosed spaces, and will often make their own changes to open arrangements for the purpose of creating protected refuges for their play (Moore, 1996).

While furniture placement is the most concrete means of delineating the boundaries of a play or work space, boundaries can also be designated through use of area rugs, tape on the floor, and curtains. The number of children who play at one time in an interest area may be subtly implied by the area's size or the number of chairs or materials provided. Limits can be more overtly stated by posting signs indicating the maximum number of children permitted in each center at one time. Some children need these more concrete guides, accompanied by frequent verbal reminders. For some children, the addition of a physical object and action to accompany entry to a center (for example, the child's personal name clip to be affixed by the child to a center availability chart) can help to make children more conscious of center participation limits. Establishing waiting lists and cultivation of other turn-taking habits can be outcomes of center-participation limits.

In addition to organizing the classroom into clearly delineated small group areas, teachers may also consider the number of "activity spaces" available within the classroom. An activity space can be defined as that occupied by a single child using a material or set of materials. For example, a large, well-equipped block area with a limit of six children can be considered as consisting of six activity areas. It has been suggested that, in order to avoid developmentally inappropriate demands for waiting, a classroom should have roughly one third more activity spaces than children (Marion, 1992). So, for a group of 20 children, there should be a minimum of 27 activity spaces. An adequate number of activity spaces may prevent the stress of too much waiting and of developmentally unrealistic demands on children's ability to share and take turns.

Much of young children's social interaction takes place in the context of social pretend play, also called "sociodramatic play." This is particularly true in the preschool and kindergarten years. Sociodramatic play continues to be important even in the primary grades (Wasserman, 2000). The most complex social play occurs in dramatic play areas (Parten, 1933; Rubin, 1977). Therefore, a simple, essential, and fundamental first step toward promoting peer interaction is to provide structured places and materials to invite such play. Because there is a higher proportion of aggression in blocks and dramatic play (Quay, Weaver, & Neel, 1986), these centers can also serve as contexts for learning to control aggressive impulses. The presence of a thoughtfully equipped block center and dramatic play (or "housekeeping") center provides important contexts for social play.

Places for Privacy

Just as social interaction and affiliation are basic human needs (Maslow, 1954), humans sometimes require a *limit* to social interaction. Privacy can also be important to healthy psychological development (Proshansky & Fabian, 1987). In the busy hubbub of an early childhood classroom, children sometimes need to retreat. Imagine yourself, as an adult, spending 8 hours in a setting akin to a child care center *without* spaces for occasional quiet individual retreat. Imagine the stress you might experience in having no opportunity to get away from 15 or 20 active and noisy peers. Imagine living this way for 5 days a week, week after week, and you may come away with an enhanced appreciation of the importance of privacy. It is no wonder that some researchers have noted that in overcrowded classrooms, children's requests to go to the bathroom increase! It seems likely that both physiological stress and desire to escape play a role.

Upon first consideration, it may seem odd to highlight the need for individual retreat in a book about promoting social interaction. Opportunities to retreat from social interaction can be important chances to regroup, refuel, and then reenter the social world with renewed energy and resources. Research has shown that children who do not have opportunities for privacy at home or at school are less competent socially and exhibit more aggressive or withdrawn behavior (Wolfe, 1978). When children are overwhelmed by the demands of continuous interaction and social exposure, they may seek to escape through crying, daydreaming, or acting out (Kostelnik et al., 2002). Some children may have greater needs for retreat and separate space than others. A basic individual difference in human personality is the distinction between introversion and extroversion. This distinction is grounded in the inclination to seek to maintain an optimal level of arousal. Simply speaking, extroverts are stimulation seekers: their threshold for social stimulation is high, and they are therefore often motivated to seek out social stimulation in order to maintain optimal arousal. Introverts are stimulation-avoiders: their threshold for social stimulation is low, and they are therefore more easily overloaded. Children who are introverts may be especially in need of self-selected opportunities to relax, self-comfort, and "get away from it all" in early childhood group settings.

Children with attention deficit disorders are also highly sensitive to overstimulation. Providing secluded, private places for individual retreat can help such children to modulate their own activity and avoid overstimulation. Many young children will not be sufficiently mature to be able to tell an adult when they are upset or exhausted or why; they may not be able to articulate to the teacher that they need to pull back. Having places for cozy private retreat available allows children to follow their own rhythms and independently retreat when they need to. This is particularly important for children with language difficulties, who are limited in their ability to "talk out" their frustrations, or for children with social competence difficulties. Children who really have to "work at" navigating the social world of the classroom, or who experience relatively frequent setbacks and frustration, may benefit from the relaxed downtime afforded by private spaces.

Figure 3.1 lists suggestions for creating private spaces in early childhood classrooms. Providing more than one such "cozy nest" in a classroom is recommended (Bunnett & Davis, 1997; Moore, 1996).

The need for privacy is likely to vary depending upon children's cultural background. Privacy tends to be more highly prized in cultures that place high value on the individual and is of lesser importance in more group-oriented cultures (Gonzalez-Mena, 1997).

Traffic Flow and Accessibility

The classroom can be arranged in a manner that all children should be able to access all areas of the classroom. Balancing this requirement with the benefits of well-delineated, protected, and cozy play spaces can present a challenge, but one that can be surmounted with a little creative thinking. The Americans with Disabilities Act (ADA) is about the issue of universal accessibility. The law requires that people with disabilities have access to the full benefits offered by an early childhood program. This means that people with disabilities must be able to access entrances, restrooms, classrooms, play spaces, and playgrounds. To prevent discrimination against

Figure 3.1. One at a Time: Designating Spaces for Private Retreat

Mattress and/or pillows in a quiet corner

Beanbag chair

Cozy closet with door removed and a curtain for privacy

Old bathtub or inflatable pool with pillows

Hammock

Overstuffed chair

Refrigerator box with cut-out door

Pup tent

Loft, or the space under a loft

people with disabilities, programs are expected to make readily achievable physical changes to accommodate those with disabilities.

Play spaces that cannot be accessed by a child with a disability send a strong message of exclusion to all of the children in the group. Efforts to promote interactions in inclusive classrooms are likely to be wasted if they are attempted on the foundation of such basic exclusionary messages. Pathways should be wide enough that a child who uses a wheelchair or walker, or children who are otherwise limited in mobility, can navigate their way around furniture and into centers. Centers should have adequate space to accommodate the child, his or her equipment, and the appropriate number of peers. If the class includes a child with visual impairment, the room should include tactile and auditory cues that the child can use to find his or her way around the classroom. Signs at the entrance to centers can include raised felt symbols indicating the center's name. A touch-distinctive sticker on the child's cubby can help him or her to find his or her place. Increased visual contrast can help the child navigate through the environment: for example, very bright tape can be used to indicate the entrance to centers. Bins for accessing and putting away manipulatves can be made readily identifiable by gluing an example of the actual object to the outside of the bin: a Lego superglued to a plastic shoebox indicates "this is the place for the Legos." Such adaptations are simple, yet can go a long way toward both helping the child with a disability feel like a full participant, and helping the other children view that child as a fully participatory member of the classroom society. The robustness of such environmental messages shouldn't be underestimated!

Center Location

The placement of interest centers should also be considered carefully. To avoid intrusion and an overabundance of conflicts, centers for quiet activities (writing, reading, and puzzles) should be located away from centers where children are likely to be louder and more active (the block center or music/movement center). Locating construction areas (art, blocks) away from frequently traveled pathways can prevent too many conflicts due to misinterpreted mishaps. This is particularly advisable in classrooms that include very young children who bump into things or who are likely to misattribute one another's intentions. It is also recommended for classrooms in which there are children with behavior disorders characterized by aggression: highly aggressive children often attribute hostile intention to other children's accidental behaviors, and often seek to retaliate (Dodge & Crick, 1990). While conflicts present important opportunities for the growth of children's social skills and social understandings, an overabundance of conflicts can become overwhelming for teachers and children alike. Careful environmental arrangements can keep conflicts to a manageable frequency.

Combining compatible play centers can also positively influence the nature of interaction. Combining the blocks and dramatic play area, or increasing their proximity, may lead to more mixed gender play (Kinsman & Berk, 1979) and potentially to more creative and divergent use of materials. Simply creating an accessible opening between two centers may lead to play partnerships that might not otherwise have happened.

AESTHETIC CONSIDERATIONS

An aesthetically pleasing environment enhances children's feelings of well-being. Children are less likely to behave aggressively when they are in a positive mood (Slaby, Roedell, Arezzo, & Hendrix, 1995). Aesthetics is the branch of philosophy that addresses beauty, creative sources and forms of art, and psychological reponses to both natural and humanmade beauty (Jalongo & Stamp, 1997). In its broadest sense, aesthetics refers to the ability to perceive through the senses (hearing, seeing, touch, smell, and taste) and to respond emotionally to what is perceived. Unfortunately, beauty is often a neglected consideration in environments for young children (Olds, 1989).

An environment that respects young children's aesthetic sensibilities can create a comfortable, relaxed, and more serene and supportive context for social interaction. Cuteness, commercialism, and cartoonish décor do not substitute for beauty. In keeping with principles of reflective teaching, view creating an aesthetically satisfying and emotionally soothing classroom context as a creative process of experimentation: Observe the results of your implemented plans. If your initial hypotheses don't seem to have been correct, reevaluate and try something else. If you who don't feel entirely comfortable as an orchestrator of aesthetic contexts, you may find it helpful to collaborate with the art teacher, the music teacher, and with parents who have particular interests or affinities in the arts, aesthetics, and creativity.

Lighting

Consider using multiple light sources as an alternative to banks of institutional fluorescent lights (spot lighting, incandescent table lamps, floor lamps, natural light). Research has demonstrated that lower lighting and light interspersed around the room is most conducive to social interaction, and when given a choice, nearly everyone prefers natural light to artificial light (Meers, 1985). Think about using a dimmer switch to control light levels: they are easy to install and not expensive.

Warmth and Softness

Soft and warm environments create security and comfort and reduce stress in young children (Weinstein, 1987). Area rugs, pillows, a cozy couch for reading, use of beautifully textured fabrics, and soft wall hangings are all ways of adding warmth and softness.

Auditory Environment

Sound control can be accomplished by providing sound-absorbing materials as recommended to add warmth and softness. Quiet, relaxing music may help to create a calm atmosphere. Many recordings of nature sounds exist (the Solitudes series is particularly extensive), including combinations of composed music and natural sounds.

Can the Clutter

Early childhood teachers are often pack rats! In an undersupported profession, we have learned to be frugal, recycle, and reuse. (At some point in my own teaching career, I had to weigh the likelihood of ever using 200 empty yogurt containers, 50 crumpled pie tins, and five wallpaper sample books against the likelihood of it all falling off the shelf and onto someone's head.) Cluttered classrooms with multiple layers of materials hung on the walls and stacks of "stored" materials on open shelves can play havoc with the child who is easily overstimulated. You might consider reserving wall space for the truly important things, like children's art work. Children's self-selected artwork hung at eye level, carefully and attractively mounted and protected, with plenty of blank wall space as backdrop sends a strong message of respect for children's individuality and creative essence. Orderliness and the serenity of some blank wall space may help the child with hyperactivity and attention difficulties to remain alert and focused.

Beautiful Things

It has been suggested that much of the psychological distress of Western civilization can be attributed to our growing "homelessness," or disconnection from nature and natural rhythms and cycles (Glendinning, 1995). To support children's connection to nature, consider inviting nature into the classroom in the following ways: nonpoisonous plants in the art area, fresh flowers on a bookcase, a basket of pinecones in the block center, seashells in the housekeeping corner, beautiful stones and pebbles displayed across a windowsill, and natural crystals hung in a window. You could incorporate some of the practices of Waldorf education, in which virtually all of children's play things are items from nature. In Waldorf programs, nature tables become small shrines for displaying and enjoying beautiful found objects of nature. Consider including as well beautiful humanmade objects of art: Pottery as a snack table centerpiece, scented potpourri at the journal table, handmade baskets to hold manipulatives, mirrors and gallery prints on the walls, wind chimes, and sculpture. An important cautionary note is to take careful stock of children's allergies and tendencies to mouth objects, when making decisions about bringing in natural items.

As you think about enhancing the aesthetic appeal of your classroom, remember that people have five senses. Take care that your aesthetic enrichments are not all visual. Individual children have preferences for different sensory modalities. Consider children with sensory impairments. A child who cannot see the playground's autumn foliage reflected in a carefully placed mirror can be soothed by the sound of a tabletop fountain. A child who does not hear the pleasant sound of a bamboo wind chime can be relaxed by the scent of cinnamon and apples potpourri.

MATERIALS AND EQUIPMENT

The kindergarten class in Room 104 hums with the activity and voices of children. A panoramic view of the classroom captures children engaged with each other, and engaged with materials of a wide variety. Crystal and Amy work in tandem on a large jigsaw puzzle. As Crystal works on locating and connecting the "edge" pieces, Amy gathers all the pieces with bright red, to piece together a hibiscus flower depicted on the puzzle box lid. The girls chat about a variety of topics, occasionally helping each other: "Here's a red that you missed." At another table, Daryl works alone on a five-piece inset puzzle, his brow furrowed in quiet and determined concentration. In the writing center, Chitra and Meghan share a plastic bin of markers, which they have placed in the center of the table. "Here's the light pink," says Chitra, handing Meghan the color she was looking for. The bin contains multiple sets of markers, enabling sharing and peer assistance in locating desired colors. A group of four children play cooperatively in the block area, using the large hollow blocks to create a houseboat. During a unit on water transportation, they have discussed the things that might be found on a houseboat. The availability of smaller unit blocks, decorative wooden blocks, and a tub of plastic dishes support the children as they create their own collective version of a houseboat. Following the 5-minutes-until-cleanup song, cleanup is accomplished in about 10 minutes as children put materials away in manageable, adequately sized and clearly marked containers on designated shelves.

Accessibility of Materials

The types and quantities of materials a teacher provides, and how these materials are presented and organized can influence the frequency, duration, and quality of children's peer interactions. Something as basic as making materials readily accessible and easy to put away can impact the development of social competence in a variety of ways. As children are able to access what they need for their work and play, they feel independent and competent. Using the classroom environment (the "third teacher") to support children's autonomy frees the teacher to function in his or her role as guide and support of children's interactions. A teacher who has to frequently step in to help children access materials (or to prevent children from accessing materials meant to be off limits) will not have the time, energy, or attention available to provide the more direct forms of support and intervention described in Chapters 4, 5, and 6. Alternatively, the teacher can encourage children's competence by:

- Arranging material on hooks, in containers, and on shelves with sufficient space that children can get them and put them back
- Using containers that all children can manage independently and successfully
- Using clear plastic containers or bins with one lower side (to allow children to see what goes in a container)
- Labeling containers with visual and/or tactile clues as to their content
- Storing, out of sight and out of reach, those materials not intended for immediate use

Quantities of Materials

Reflective teachers make important decisions about numbers and varieties of materials to provide. Too many options in the classroom can cause children to become overwhelmed and to flit from one option to another without becoming engaged. Too few materials can lead to conflict and quarreling. It has been suggested that the total number of play units should be 2 1/2 times the number of children: a play unit is defined as an object or set of objects needed by one child to use it effectively (Kostelnik et al., 2002). Some research has shown that limiting the amount of materials encourages sharing, thereby increasing interaction (Smith & Connelly, 1980) and increasing expressive language (Hart & Risley, 1980). At the same time, teachers are often advised to provide more than one of the most fervently sought high-interest items, especially for developmentally young children. Seemingly conflicting evidence can lead to confusing or oversimplified advice. Perhaps the important lesson to be learned about numbers of materials to provide is "It matters, and it depends." As a teacher views the interactions in her or his classroom, and considers the goals she or he wants to meet for individual children and for the group as a whole, she or he is in the best position to make and test hypotheses about numbers of particular items to provide, in order to support and encourage children's developing abilities to share and take turns.

Social Materials

Providing materials and toys that have been specifically chosen to encourage social, rather than isolate, play can increase the rate of interaction between children with and without disabilities. This effect is most pronounced for children with disabilities (Quilitch & Risley, 1973; Rettig, Kallam, & McCarthy-Salm, 1993).

Most of the research in this area has been done with preschool children. Studies suggest that blocks, dishes, dolls, and housekeeping equipment have high potential to elicit social play. Art activities, books, puzzles, Peg-Boards, parquetry blocks, and toy animals elicited more solitary or parallel play. Fluid and malleable materials, such as play dough, clay, sand, and water, have sometimes been observed to contribute to social play but have been shown in other studies to contribute to isolate play. Equipment can be described along a dimension of simple to complex. Complex units can be used in a greater variety of ways than can simple materials. Children tend to play cooperatively with complex play units, while simple units elicit greater solitary or parallel play (Charlesworth & Hartup, 1967; Hendrickson, Strain, Tremblay, & Shores, 1981; Kostelnik et al., 2002; Rubin, 1977; Stoneman, Cantrell, & Hoover-Dempsey, 1983; Van Alstyne, 1932).

Teachers will, of course, want to provide a variety of both social and isolate materials, and simple and complex units. When teachers manipulate the availability of materials for the purpose of increasing social interaction, they can rely on their own observations of the particular children between whom they are attempting to increase interaction, and the types of activities within which modification of materials is likely to change interaction. An intervention as simple as adding a second telephone to the dramatic play center, putting dolls in the block center, or adding a wok and Chinese cooking utensils to the housekeeping corner may positively affect the complexity and duration of social play.

Contexts for Sociodramatic Play

As noted earlier, a great deal of young children's social interaction takes place through the medium of make believe. Two classroom centers in which much of this type of play occurs are the block center and the housekeeping or dramatic play center. For these reasons, providing well-equipped and enticing block and dramatic play centers is an important component of promoting peer interaction. Because children's pretend play is not confined to indoor areas, teachers may also consider providing dramatic play props and blocks on the playground (on a patio, at the sandbox, in an adult-constructed playhouse or child-constructed fort) (Perry, 2001).

Social pretend play puts special demands on young children's cognitive and language skills. When dramatic play involves more than one child, children have to negotiate roles and "story lines"; they need to have some ability to communicate about the play. Selection of materials that encourage complex and extended dramatic play can be tied to a thematic unit: If the theme for the month is community helpers, provision of related props will allow children to build and extend their understanding of the concepts and information included in the unit. Tying dramatic play props to a unit of study helps to ensure that children have some common ground from which to build their pretend play. In the same way, props linked to stories that are enjoyed by the group can provide common ground. If children have a rich array of common ground and supportive props upon which to build their play, they may be even less likely to spend their time engaged in stereotypical or scripted play drawn from television programs (which often include aggressive content). Howe (1993) has found significantly more pretend play in familiar dramatic play centers such as the bakery or grocery store. Linking these centers to a unit on grocery stores can help to make them even more familiar to children, and easier for children to develop their play together. Furthermore, linking the materials in the housekeeping center to the real artifacts of children's gender and cultural backgrounds also helps to familiarize the setting. Consider providing a tortilla press and play dough, a mortar and pestle, a *rakweh* (long-handled Arabic coffeepot) and small Arabic coffee cups, and dress-up clothes that appeal to boys as well those that appeal to girls. As with other aspects of the classroom environment (photos and art on walls, characters in books, dolls), the materials provided should convey respect for a diversity of people, and particular sensitivity to the background of the children in the class.

Materials throughout the classroom can be selected to reflect a wide variety of abilities and racial, cultural, and socioeconomic backgrounds.

TIME, SCHEDULES, AND ROUTINES

As teachers plan the daily schedule, they make decisions about what kinds of activities are included, how much time is apportioned for particular activity periods within the schedule, and how much flexibility the schedule will allow. Some teachers, of course, have more freedom and latitude than others do in this regard. However, even primary grade teachers in large and highly structured public schools can work with administrators and other colleagues to get the best schedule for the children in their class. When a teacher can articulate her or his reasons for desiring a particular schedule change, can explain the schedule's relationship to important goals for children, and can simultaneously acknowledge some of the reasons that other stakeholders (administrators, other colleagues) may have for the currently imposed schedule, she or he is in a better position to work cooperatively with others to create a feasible schedule accommodation.

As teachers consider the organization of time in their program, their decision making can be guided by their past experiences and accumulated wisdom, by their knowledge of the children they teach, and by the findings of research. Research evidence suggests that children engage in more peer interaction during less structured activities than during formally structured activities (Sainato & Carta, 1992). One such study found that the highest rates of verbal social interaction for both children with and without disabilities occurred during free play and cleanup time (Odom, Peterson, McConnell, & Ostrosky, 1990). The specific types of less structured activities that are most conducive to peer interaction may differ for children with and without disabilities. Another study found that children without disabilities interacted most during free play, while children with disabilities interacted most during snack time (Kohl & Beckman, 1984). Furthermore, the specific nature of "free play" seems to make a difference. Some research indicates that, for children with disabilities, play activities in which teachers provide some structure by setting rules, establishing a theme, and assigning roles are the play activities in which the highest rates of interaction occurred (DeKlyen & Odom, 1989). Though research on the optimal amount of free play is limited, evidence suggests that children will engage in more mature and complex levels of play during longer play periods (Tegano & Burdette, 1991). Large blocks of time allow children to develop engrossing play ideas and to work through challenging interactions. Frequent changes of activity may not allow children sufficient time to collaborate on the completion of tasks (Gareau & Kennedy, 1991) or to engage in complex and satisfying play. Based on their research with typically developing children, Christie and Wardle (1992) have suggested that a minimum of 30 minutes be allotted for free play. On the other hand, McEvoy, Fox, and Rosenberg (1991) have suggested that for many children with disabilities, the schedule can be divided into short time segments, depending on the activity and the length of the child's attention.

Though seemingly complicated and potentially contradictory, such evidence need not leave teachers in a quandary. Studies such as those cited above suggest several useful implications for practice. First, since freeplay and cleanup time provide important opportunities for peer interaction, teachers who are concerned with optimally promoting peer interaction skills will want to observe their children carefully to gauge the maximum appropriate amount of time to allot to these activities, and will want to structure their own activity so that they are available to facilitate interaction as needed during these two times during the daily schedule. Simply considering that cleanup time is more than only a time to put things away, but rather is also a time for cooperative verbal interaction, can encourage a teacher to reexamine the nature of his or her role during this period.

Teachers whose class includes children with widely varying levels of maturity and ability can accommodate different needs by providing, for example, a 40-minute free play period within which the time can be broken up for children who require more frequent change of activity, and during which the level of structure varies by activity. Consider the following example:

Ms. Karsten's kindergarten group is comprised of 18 5- and 6-year-olds, including 6-year-old Kaylee who has mental retardation. Each morning, Ms. Karsten provides a 40-minute free choice period during which children are allowed to engage in any of the centers included in the classroom: The housekeeping center, the block center, the basic art and writing center, the book center, the sand table, or the science center. Children are free to visit as few or as many centers as they choose during the 40-minute time, but must comply with the posted limits regarding the number of children allowed in each center. Ms. Karsten has noted that individual children's patterns of engagement vary. Thomas and Martin, for example, often choose to spend all of their time in the block area becoming engrossed in collaborative fantasy play surrounding their various construction projects. Janelle and Jim are more likely to visit two or three centers during the 40 minutes; while Sarah, Sam, and Erin typically engage briefly but productively in four or five centers. Kaylee, if left to her own resources, would usually begin in the dramatic play area, but her solitary play there would become disorganized and disruptive after 5 or 10 minutes. Ms. Karsten recognizes that she needs to structure Kaylee's time and activity during free play. At the beginning of free play, she and Kaylee sit down with a planning board and identify three or four activities in which Kaylee would like to participate during free play. As Kaylee participates, Ms. Karsten watches her for signs that she needs extra support to extend her play, and for signs that it is time to move on to another activity. Pointing to the planning board, she says, "Kaylee, remember you wanted blocks. Finish here. Let me help you go to blocks."

Ms. Karsten also plans two or three structured play activities for Kaylee to participate in during free play each week. She may, for example, provide a tortilla press and play dough in the housekeeping area, and engage Kaylee and two other children in playing tortilla factory for 5 minutes or so. She says, "Let's have a tortilla factory. Suzette, we need someone to make the balls of dough and put them in this basket for Kaylee. Kaylee, put a ball on the press like this . . . . Now press. Kim can be in charge of putting the tortilla in the frying pan." In this way, Ms. Karsten has created an embedded structure for Kaylee, within the more open structure provided for other children. By doing this, she can help Kaylee organize and manage her play time, and has opportunities to provide support and instruction to Kaylee as needed.

Snack time is often noted to be an important occasion for social interaction between peers. Evidence that this may be an especially important social time for children with disabilities, coupled with the evidence that children without disabilities do not often choose to interact with children who have disabilities, suggests that a formal sit-down snack time is particularly important in an inclusive classroom. Group snack times can be considered in contrast to the increasingly visible "fast food" version of snack time, in which a snack is provided as a center choice during center time, which children visit at will and sometimes one at a time. Providing for a relaxed, family-style snack time gives children a chance to practice their social skills in the absence of materials and activities as mediators of interaction. Such conversational time also provides children a chance to practice manners, in the presence and with the support of an adult or adults who sit down and enjoy snack and conversation with the children.

Research on primary grade children's social behavior at lunch and during play is limited. Observation suggests, however, that in today's climate of increasing academic pressure, lunch and recess are the times when the bulk of children's peer interaction occurs. Unfortunately, however, the typical public school lunchroom is loud and crowded. Playground time has become a thing of the past in some schools, and has been abbreviated in many others (Clements, 2001). Some enterprising teachers take children outdoors to eat lunch, or allow them to eat in the relative peace and quiet of the classroom, sometimes foregoing their own daily "break time" to do so. If a morning snack is not provided by the school district, some teachers organize parents to cooperate in sending food, allowing children to have a relaxed time to chat in addition to a midmorning energy boost. A collaborative brainstorming session involving parents, administrators, teachers, and perhaps students and cafeteria workers, as well, may result in creative solutions. Finding a way to restore or protect the relaxed social character of meal times may be more easily accomplished if all participants are helped to acknowledge how important this basic comfort is to them personally.

HUMAN ENVIRONMENT: THE PEOPLING OF THE PROGRAM

Who is here? Another aspect of environment is the people present as part of that environment. The number of children comprising the class, the number of adults present in relation to the number of children, the amount of space available per individual, and the diversity of individuals included in the group, are all characteristics of the human environment.

Ratio and Group Size

Substantial evidence supports the relevance of the adult-child ratio to early childhood program quality (Howes & Hamilton, 1993). It is reasonable to expect that the extent and nature of teachers' support of children's peer interactions may be enhanced or constrained by the number of children for whom a teacher has responsibility and the number of adults available to assist. My research has indicated that a higher ratio of adults to children is associated with the use of teacher interventions having high potential to help children become autonomous in negotiating successful peer interaction, while low adult-child ratios are associated with the use of disruptive and punitive teacher interventions (Kemple, David, & Hysmith, 1997).

Adult-child ratio should also be considered in the context of overall group size. While an adult-child ratio of one adult to ten children may be appropriate for a class of 4-year-old children, it would not be appropriate to populate a class with three adults and thirty 4-year-olds. The social demands of getting to know, feel comfortable with, and feel a measure of predictability in a group of 30 peers is likely to be overwhelming for the typical 4-year-old, and crushing for the child with significant social difficulties. At the same time, the adults' ability to adequately know 30 individual young children for the purposes of supporting their social growth in individually appropriate ways would be highly questionable.

The National Association for the Education of Young Children (NAEYC) has suggested guidelines for adult-child ratio, group size, and staff qualifications. Optimum group size for children in the primary grades is identified as 15 to 18 children with one adult, or up to 25 children with a second adult. Kindergarten groups should not exceed 25 children with two adults, 4-year-olds should be in groups of no more than 20 with two adults, and 3-year-olds should be in groups of no more than 16 with two adults. Teachers of 3- to 5-year-olds should have college-level preparation in early childhood education or child development, and supervised experience with this age group. Teachers of 6- to 8-year-olds should have supervised field experience with this age group and be qualified through early childhood education degree programs, or through elementary degree programs with a concentrated course of study in early childhood education (Bredekamp & Copple, 1997).

Social Density

Social density refers to the number of individuals in relation to the physical area of the classroom space. Space should be adequate, but not too large. It seems that if space is too large, there is limited social contact among children, while if space is too small, the rate of aggressive behavior increases. Based upon reviews of the research literature it has been suggested that 25 square feet of classroom activity space per child should be the minimum space available. When spatial density of 15 square feet of classroom space per child is reached, evidence suggests more occurrences of negative and inappropriate behavior (Smith & Connolly, 1980).

Inclusion

Finally, as discussed in Chapter 1, the simple fact of inclusion also lays an important foundation for the development of peer skills, social understanding, and relationships for children with and without disabilities. The availability of peers who can serve as models and initiators of social interaction is asserted as an important rationale for including children with disabilities in classrooms with typically developing peers (McGregor & Vogelsberg, 1998). The principle of "natural proportions" is the often repeated suggestion that children with disabilities should be included in numbers proportionate to the presence of individuals with disabilities in the population at large, which would suggest that a typically sized early childhood classroom of 15 to 25 students include one or two children with disabilities. Some empirical support exists to suggest that the proportion of typical children to children with disabilities may indeed impact peer social interaction (Guralnick & Groom, 1988).

Social competence and communication skills of children with disabilities may improve when they are educated in inclusive settings where peers can serve as models and as sources of natural reinforcement. There is evidence that friendship networks of children with disabilities are more extensive in inclusive settings than in self-contained special education classes. The presence of children with disabilities creates opportunities for typically developing children to learn about issues of fairness and equity. In one investigation, even children in kindergarten in an inclusive school exhibited sophisticated concepts of fairness and were able to describe principles of equal treatment (McGregor & Vogelsberg, 1998).

Attention to the number of children in a classroom, the inclusion of children with varying abilities, as well as the availability of sensitive adults and adequate space, can influence the social possibilities for that classroom setting. The potential for supporting friendship and competent interaction is colored by "who is here."

EMOTIONAL CLIMATE: THE AFFECTIVE ENVIRONMENT

Twenty-five second graders are seated in a bunch on the floor. Mrs. Ruiz sits on a small chair, reading from a chapter book. Without missing a beat, she looks up from her reading and says with a note of excitement, anticipation, and importance, "In five minutes Jeffrey will go to reading." She then immediately resumes her reading. Jeffrey goes daily for reading tutoring down the hall, always accompanied on the journey by a peer. Today will be his first day to walk down the hall all by himself, a feat about which he is proud, excited, and a bit apprehensive. Mrs. Ruiz finishes Chapter 3 and says, "It is time for reading, Jeffrey." A small ripple of excitement seems to move across the group as they turn toward Jeffrey. As Jeffrey, who has Down syndrome, stands and turns toward the door, his second grade classmates break into spontaneous applause! Jeffrey beams as he walks out the door.

How has such a climate of caring and community come to exist in this group of 7-, 8-, and 9-year-old children? An atmosphere of this sort rarely happens spontaneously. As Mrs. Ruiz says, "You better *believe* this was intentional. I *work* at this!"

Several weeks later, the same group of children is on a field trip to a park. Jeffrey trudges off toward the ball field, his arms entwined in a shoulder hug of solidarity with two of his buddies. One of his classmates (a quiet and popular boy who leaves class daily to attend a program for children who are "intellectually gifted") wistfully confides to an adult, "I'd like to be friends with Jeffrey, but he already has so many friends."

So far, this chapter has examined many concrete elements of classroom environment that support the development of peer competence and relationships. The less tangible elements of a supportive classroom environment also contribute importantly to the success of the more directed strategies that will be described in the following chapters. A positive emotional atmosphere conveys fundamentally important messages to children: "This is a place you can trust." "This is a caring place." "*You* belong here."

"This Is a Place You Can Trust"

The necessity of creating a classroom climate of trust and dependability is more critical than ever, and is also more difficult than it ever was in the past. Many young children enter early childhood programs without the expectation that their world is a safe place, a predictable place, a helpful place (Hyson, 1994). When children come to school from environments that have not helped them develop a sense of security and trust, it is particularly important that teachers work to make the classroom a safe and predictable place (Howes & Ritchie, 2002).

Predictability and safety are conveyed when teachers follow a predictable schedule, one that is posted and visible and understood by the children. A daily time line accompanied by pictures representing the day's activity periods and routines can be "read" even by very young children. Predictability and safety are conveyed when teachers make their expectations for children's behavior very clear. Creation of a few basic classroom rules, frequent contextualized reminders of rules, and explicit instruction in how to enact the rules and routines can help children feel secure in knowing what they are supposed to do. This means that discipline is viewed as a process of teaching appropriate behaviors and reasons for rules. In essence, clear expression of expectations means teaching children "what to do" rather than merely admonishing them about what not to do. In a safe and trustworthy environment, children are taught rules, routines, and reasons; are given encouragement and supported opportunities to comply with expectations; and are warned in advance of reasonable and meaningful consequences that will occur if they do not behave appropriately after a warning. An individually appropriate approach to discipline recognizes that some children may need more direct programs of systematic reinforcement and inhibiting consequences than do others (Duncan, Kemple, &

Smith, 2000). Description of an individually appropriate and age-appropriate system of guidance and discipline is beyond the scope of this book, yet it lays essential groundwork for the development of positive interactions and peer relationships. Good sources of explicit information on this topic are Kostelnik et al. (2002) and Zirpoli (1995).

"This Is a Caring Place"

A national survey asked parents and children what characteristic they most prize in a teacher. Parents identified the teacher's ability to motivate children to learn as the characteristic they value most. What did children have to say? Children indicated that what they most desired from a teacher was his or her respectful care and concern (Boyer, 1995). Research supports the idea that when a young child's relationship with the teacher is characterized by warmth and security, the child can use the teacher as resource for other relationships, including peer relationships (Howes & Ritchie, 2002). In essence, the child may use the teacher as a secure base from which to venture out and explore peer relationships. Teachers can create a climate of caring by acknowledging and accepting children's emotions while teaching them appropriate avenues for emotional expression. Teachers can model empathy and encourage children's empathic responses to peers. Sending cards to a child who is absent due to an extended illness is one way teachers and children can respond empathetically together. Modeling consolation and encouragement for a child who has been disappointed, and celebrating individual successes are other ways teachers can teach empathy. Use of "other-oriented" reasoning, in which adults help children identify the impact of their behavior on others, is another way to create a climate of caring.

When a teacher makes a point of having a few seconds to greet each child early in the day, he or she has an opportunity to touch base and take each child's "emotional temperature." Such checkup times can help the teacher identify those children who may need extra support or TLC on a particular day. In the primary grades, teachers sometimes keep ongoing dialog journals with individual children as a means of maintaining open lines of communication about children's concerns. In the preschool and kindergarten years, affective and behavioral reflection ("You seem sad." "I see you standing all alone.") are gentle ways of expressing interest in children's feelings and inviting communication in a noninvasive way.

"You Belong Here"

When teachers help to create a culture that recognizes each child as an individual and which is sensitive to each child's uniqueness, and when teachers encourage children to embrace the diversity within the world of their classroom and school, they help convey the message that each child matters and each child belongs. When teachers help to create an atmosphere of groupness, interdependence, and community, children hear the message, "We *all* belong here, together."

Uniqueness, individuality, and diversity can be celebrated in many ways: some very simple, some more elaborate. Using children's names, using them frequently, and pronouncing them properly and without hesitation communicates recognition of the individual and helps children learn one another's names. Neglecting to accord children this basic respect makes a shaky foundation upon which to build a "diversity curriculum" or a "multicultural approach." Providing each child with a protected space (a cubby) for their belongings conveys that their important "stuff" from home will be safe.

Each child's uniqueness can be celebrated through "special day" traditions. The children in the "fours class" with Ms. Starsky and Ms. Jones each enjoy their own special day about once every 8 weeks. On a child's special day, his or her family is invited to provide a simple snack for the class. The special-day child can bring an item from home, or choose an item from the classroom, to hide in the special-day mystery box. At the morning circle, the child provides three clues as to the content of the mystery box, and classmates eagerly guess. The special-day child sits up in the big rocking chair at the morning circle, and tells several important things about himself or herself, with teachers' prompting and support if needed; for example, "My whole name is Rasha Mari Berbari, I have a brother named Samir, I love cats and chocolate. I can speak English and Arabic. I am going camping with my Baba and my brother on the weekend." Primary grade children can participate in "mystery person of the day," a practice in which the mystery child secretly provides several little-known facts about himself or herself and classmates guess the mystery person's identity. These are useful alternatives to the traditional show-and-tell experience in which multiple children speak more or less uncomfortably about a toy from home, while the audience fidgets and neglects to listen. Another variation on show and tell is word-a-day practices, through which children "bring" to school a word, phrase, or saying that is somewhat unique to their family or to their family's culture.

Acceptance of children's family, language, and culture is conveyed when familiar artifacts of each child's background are present in the classroom, and when classroom materials (books, pictures, music, and so forth) represent the ethnicity, culture, language, economic status, and special needs of all children in the class. Paints, markers, and crayons in various flesh tones allow children to represent themselves and their families without having to sacrifice their true colors. A strong message of acceptance is conveyed when families are warmly and regularly included through friendly interactions at arrival and departure time, brief opportunities to dialog through a weekly communication journal, and an open-door classroom policy.

"We Belong Here"

At 4, Sari was a shy, quiet member of her class group. Toward the end of the school year, several class books from previous years were displayed in the reading center. Sari flipped through the pages of an album depicting a bean garden project from 2 years earlier. To her apparent amazement, she discovered several photographs of her older brother Nathan engaged in the gardening project. She picked up the album and traveled purposefully around the classroom with it, proudly announcing to numerous peers, "That's my big brother." With unmistakable awe and uncharacteristic audibility, she added, "He used to be in this class."

This act of initiative on Sari's part was unusual. Approaching peers with something novel and personal to share was not a typical behavior for Sari, and as I observed this, I wondered what might have happened had this album been present in the reading center early in the year. Would Nathan's photographic presence in her new class have made a difference in Sari's initial adjustment? Would this concrete and visible symbol of the intersecting rings of family and classroom community have increased her comfort in a substantial way?

The album depicting the bean gardening project was created by Nathan's teacher as a means of immortalizing an important chapter in the life of her community of 4- and 5-year-old children. Making memories, making memories tangible, and thereby making memories readily accessible to young children is an important means of building a sense of community history. Sari's serendipitous discovery of this historical document highlights the utility of considering communities as concentric and intersecting rings: classroom community is embedded within the larger school community as well as within a string of communities that came before inside those same four walls.

A feeling of community, of being part of an interdependent group entity, can be created through some fairly basic practices. Documenting classroom life through class memory albums and preserving group projects through collaboratively created group memory walls and bulletin boards are important ways of memorializing the social experiences of a classroom group. Such palpable reminders of social activity help to underscore that the classroom group is more than a collection of individual members. The classroom community is greater than the sum of its parts, and concrete reminders help make this salient to young children.

The calendar can be used as a means of helping children appreciate shared class history. Instead of using "calendar time" only for teaching number sequences, the days of the week sequence, and patterning, teachers can make calendar time a meaningful lesson in recent history. Some teachers select a different child each day to draw or represent in some way a significant event in the life of the class that occurs on that day. At day's end that small picture can be affixed to the calendar (a drawing of a pizza on the day the class made pizzas; a drawing of curtains and a stage on the day they watched the fifth graders' play; and so forth). At the end of the month, calendar squares can be cut apart and affixed one per page to an album in which children may write and dictate their recollections of particular days. By the end of the year, the classroom library may contain nine or ten such calendar albums, which children can browse to revisit their shared history.

"Morning meeting," problem-solving meetings, sharing circle, and so forth are means of creating a feeling of community. A morning circle time can commence with a greeting song that recognizes individual children, and tells them "we're each here and part of something bigger than ourselves." Traditional greeting songs in which each child's name is mentioned, such as "The More We Get Together" provide children with an opportunity to look at, say the names of, and recognize the presence of each individual peer, as well as to be on the receiving end of gaze and recognition. A gradually built repertoire of songs enjoyed by the group of children and sung frequently have great potential to build a sense of "groupness" in the context of a relaxed pleasant experience: We are friends when we sing together. Circle rituals in which children each have the opportunity to share something that is bothering them, something about which they are excited, or simply "I'm fine" or "I don't want to share" can serve as an emotional checkup by which the teacher can gauge individual needs and group interaction at the beginning of the day, and demonstrate and encourage empathic response and caring. Regular problem-solving circles give children an opportunity to raise problems regarding classroom life, and to participate together in seeking solutions.

SUMMARY

The classroom context sets a stage for the development of children's peer social skills and peer relationships. Classroom ecology consists of the temporal environment, the concrete physical environment, and the affective atmosphere. The daily schedule sequence, amounts of time allotted to activities and routines that serve as important settings for peer interaction, the arrangement of the classroom into centers, selection and display of materials, classroom décor, lighting, and availability of peer models and caring supportive adults are among the setting factors that can influence the social climate of the classroom. A thoughtfully constructed classroom environment can provide the context which encourages and supports children's emerging peer competence. I have described several aspects of classroom environment that may impact social relationships. The creation of a supportive context requires an ongoing process of reflection. As teachers create the environment that works for their students, they are likely to find that a well-designed environment can serve as an additional "teacher," allowing children's maximum autonomy, freeing the human teachers from unnecessary management tasks and rendering them available to support children's peer interactions via more directed and intensive interventions as needed.

FOOD FOR THOUGHT

1. Consider the list of social competencies provided below. For each competency, try to create an exhaustive list of ways the environment can support attainment of those competencies. Think beyond the direct and obvious!

   Organizing play with peers
   Sharing play materials with peers
   Engaging in conversations with peers
   Taking turns with peers
   Providing assistance to peers
   Engaging in conversation with peers
   Cooperating with peers
   Respecting peers' differences

2. Imagine that a child who uses a wheelchair is joining your class. This child has full use of his upper body, but cannot walk. How could you use the temporal, physical, and emotional environment to support the full inclusion of this child in your classroom community? Think of as many environmental support strategies as you can. How might your strategies differ if your class were gaining a child with a severe hearing impairment instead? A child who is blind? A child who is very sensitive to sensory stimulation

CHAPTER 4

Naturalistic Strategies to Promote Peer Interaction and Social Inclusion

NATURALISTIC STRATEGIES are those that are integrated within the natural flow of classroom activity. When the stage has been set with the environmental arrangements and climate creation described in Chapter 3, the classroom becomes the arena within which adults can support, intervene in, and sometimes orchestrate the drama of children's social activity. Naturalistic interventions can be easily embedded in ongoing classroom routines and activities and require minimum adult effort and time. They are therefore more likely to be considered feasible by teachers and to be implemented consistently (Odom et al., 1993). Interventions that are implemented by teachers during routine classroom activities can help to overcome two major problems that are often associated with more direct, structured social interaction interventions: lack of generalization of social behavior to other contexts, and lack of teacher implementation (Brown, Ragland, & Fox, 1988; McEvoy et al., 1988). In this chapter, on-the-spot teaching strategies and the process of conflict mediation will be described. Chapter 5 will describe the slightly more structured forms of naturalistic interventions.

"ON-THE-SPOT" SUPPORT

Social skills are learned and practiced primarily through interactive processes: through the give and take of peer play and work. Intervention offered by teachers in a natural context provides young children the opportunity to interact with something meaningful to them, while in the presence of adults who are available to suggest social strategies appropriate to the specific context in which they are to be applied (Katz & McClellan, 1997). In the early childhood years, one of the most useful social interventions may be the spontaneous coaching and modeling that many teachers do almost continually within the natural context of school activities and routines (Ramsey, 1991).

Facilitation in the naturalistic context of ongoing interaction has been suggested by many in the field of general early childhood education to be the most advantageous approach. This form of intervention has recently received increasing attention in the early childhood special education literature. On-the-spot teaching is conducted during unstructured activities for brief periods of time, typically within the context of children's involvement in self-initiated activities. As the field of early childhood special education has expanded its theoretical base to incorporate a developmental framework, interest has expanded in interventions embedded in the ongoing routines and activities of classroom life (see Bricker, Pretti-Frontczak, & McComas, 1998; Guralnick, 1993). There is growing sentiment among professionals in early childhood special education that naturalistic strategies be tried before considering more teacher-directed approaches such as social skills training groups and direct teacher reinforcement of desired social behaviors (Conroy, Langenbrunner, & Burleson, 1996).

Spontaneous Teaching

Teachers can offer young children on-the-spot support in the context of ongoing natural peer interaction. This may be done spontaneously, whenever the teacher observes an opportunity to guide children through a difficult interaction that they do not seem able to negotiate independently. For example, as described in the illustrations below, over the course of a single morning Mr. McDonald may encounter numerous opportunities to facilitate challenging interactions among children who are relatively socially competent but who appear to need a little help in a discrete circumstance.

During morning meeting, Daryl and Diantre are squabbling over who gets to sit on the blue carpet square. When it appears that the squabble will not be independently solved in a timely fashion (Mr. McDonald has 18 other kindergartners ready for meeting, and they need to be in the music room in 30 minutes), he prompts the boys by saying, "What are you going to do about this? There is only one blue carpet square, but a lot of other colors are available." In this case, the prompt (and Mr. McDonald's attention) are enough to enable a solution to this conflict of possession. Diantre releases the carpet square with a sigh, and finds another.

Thirty minutes later, on the way to the music room, Mia (who has been assigned to hold the door open as her classmates pass through) has a moment of distraction. She allows the door to fall closed as Suki, the last in line, is about to enter the room. Suki lets out a mournful wail from the other side of the closed door. Mr. McDonald guides Mia back to the door, opens it, and waits a moment to see what the girls will do. Mia looks vacantly at Suki, who continues a forced, feeble wail. Quickly assessing the situation (and employing a little educated guesswork), Mr. McDonald says to Suki, "I'm not sure Mia noticed what she did!" Suki says nothing, and Mia looks distracted. Mr. McDonald says, "Mia, look at Suki's face. Suki, tell Mia what happened." "You slammed the door!" sniffs Suki. Mia giggles, "Ooops. I'm sorry." Mr. McDonald says lightly, "Being the door holder is an important job—you've got to make sure all the ducks are through the door before you close it!" He restates to Suki, "She didn't know you were there." In this episode, Mr. McDonald has served as an interpreter, prompting the two girls to recognize one another's perspective. He helped Suki to see that Mia harbored no hostile intent, and helped Mia to recognize how her inattention had caused Suki to feel snubbed.

Later that morning during free play, Christine and Jen are painting a floor mural, using pie tins of thinned tempera paint. Christine accidentally puts her knee on the edge of one pan, splashing orange paint up into her face and onto her smock and clothing. As Christine cries in frustration, Mr. McDonald notices that Jen is immobilized and appears genuinely distressed by her friend's predicament. With one arm around Christine, he says gently to Jen, "You can help her out by getting some damp paper towels." With Christine's permission, Mr. McDonald shows Jen how she can help Christine get cleaned up. Here, Mr. McDonald has helped Jen respond to her friend's need in a prosocial way. While Jen may have noted an opportunity to offer assistance and wanted to help, the drama of the moment had rendered her unable to figure out *how* to help.

Finally, at lunch, Mr. McDonald eavesdrops as Clarence, Jacob, and Celine compare notes about the burdensome nature of younger siblings.

Their assertions like "My baby sister always wrecks everything," "My brother lost half of my Legos," and "I'm going to dig a moat so my dumb sister can't ever get in my room," escalate to a fevered pitch. Suddenly, the three are loudly interrupting one another as they vie for the title of most-martyred sibling. Mr. McDonald de-escalates the situation by sitting down briefly with them, touching each on the forearm, and reflecting, "Sounds like you all have problems with babies. So many problems, everyone wants to talk at the same time." He then models rapt listening behaviors as he asks the three in turn to share further stories. When Celine says, "Once my sister tore up my best picture of a rainbow," Mr. McDonald scaffolds a connection to Jacob's earlier utterance, saying, "that sounds like your frustrating problem, Jacob—you said your baby sister wrecks things." After a couple more referrals to help the children attend to one another, Mr. McDonald withdraws to once again listen from a distance as the children proceed with a more mannerly discussion.

In all of these interactions, Mr. McDonald seized the moment by offering impromptu facilitation. Though none of these children happened to be children with significant deficits in social competence, they were all *young children*. Young children are engaged in a long and gradual process of developing the skills, knowledge, and dispositions of competent social interaction. Even the most socially sophisticated young child can benefit from a teacher's perceptive intervention from time to time.

Planned "Incidental Teaching"

Incidental teaching is conducted planfully, when the teacher has identified particular social competence goals for an individual child who may benefit from targeted naturalistic support. Conroy and Brown (2002) suggest that teachers identify common activities and circumstances that will allow the teacher to use incidental teaching strategies (e.g., free play, center time, snack time, and arrival time). These less-structured times will allow the teacher more freedom to observe and intervene, plan a variety of methods to encourage peer interactions through physical or verbal guidance, and then provide encouragement and support when peer interactions occur. Let's examine a scenario in which some of these suggestions are put into action.

Ms. Katrina has detected a dilemma regarding 4-year-old Perry's social integration in play and conversation [recall the definition of an experienced dilemma from Chapter 2, and its role as the initial point in the cycle of reflective teaching]. Ms. Katrina has noted that Perry joins into play and con-

versation readily, but her involvement is rarely maintained for more than
a few minutes. After careful observation, Ms. Katrina notices that Perry's
responses to her peers' utterances are often "noncontingent"—that is, she
very frequently responds off-topic, saying things that are unrelated to her
peers' expressed ideas. For example, at the snack table the three children
seated with Perry are talking about what has been served and whether
they like it: "Broccoli is my favorite." "My dad always makes it with
cheesy sauce." "I like to eat broccoli, but it smells yuck." In the midst of
ongoing broccoli-talk, Perry chimes in with, "I can't ride the escalator if I
have the red ones on." Perry is ignored, and the broccoli talk continues
for another moment or two.

Perry's egocentric topic changes are also evident in pretend play situations. For example, several children are engrossed in the dramatic play
corner, developing a play scenario involving hiding under a table with
money and jewels, to escape from an imaginary witch. "Quick, hide them
here!" "The witch is flying down, hurry!" "I'll sit on the money so she
can't see it." Perry, Grace, Janine, and Sue scramble excitedly under the
table. As Grace, Janine, and Sue whisper warnings of impending danger
in tones of barely contained exuberance, Perry crawls out from under the
table, gets a large bowl, and crawls back under, saying, "Now let's make
the salad too," as she grabs the play money from beneath Grace's derriere
and transforms the green bills into lettuce leaves. A conflict erupts. "That's
our money, we're hiding it from the witch. Give it." As the girls argue, the
play falls apart. Grace, Janine, and Sue resume their witch theme only
after Perry leaves the area.

Ms. Katrina has observed numerous situations such as these, in which
Perry demonstrates difficulty maintaining a topic of play or conversation
because she does not respond in ways that are clearly connected to the
motives, interests, and ideas of her playmates. Ms. Katrina understand
the natural egocentrism that is part of being a 4-year-old, and recognizes
that Perry is developmentally more egocentric than many of her peers.
Ms. Katrina also recognizes that "topic changes" in conversation and play
are important, part of what keeps things rolling, makes interaction interesting, and enables the evolution of exciting play ideas. But Perry's topic
changes are radical, abrupt, and frequent. They are impeding her ability
to participate in peer interaction. While she recognizes that Perry's egocentrism may limit the extent to which her topic maintenance behavior
can change, Ms. Katrina believes that she can help Perry make sufficient
behavioral and social-cognitive progress to enable her to be better integrated into play and conversation, and to enjoy the camaraderie afforded
by greater social inclusion.

What has occurred so far in this illustration? The teacher has identified a child (Perry) who can benefit from some naturalistic assistance in interacting appropriately with peers. She has identified a particular area of social competence (topic maintenance) as one with which Perry needs help. With regard to the reflective teaching cycle presented in Chapter 2, she has identified a dilemma and defined a problem.

Next, Ms. Katrina thinks about common activities and circumstances that will allow her to use incidental teaching strategies. She decides to pay special attention to Perry's social behavior during snack time and free play. Because Perry's difficulty involves topic maintenance, snack time is a logical circumstance to target as an intervention context, since snack time is generally a time of relaxed small group conversations in this class. Ms. Katrina typically sits with a small snack group while her assistant moves back and forth among the other three snack tables. This will afford Ms. Katrina an excellent opportunity to tune in to and support Perry through incidental teaching. Free play time will also be a good context to target for incidental teaching. Perry usually chooses to start her free play time in the dramatic play center, an area that is designed to elicit interactive pretend play as well as communication about play.

The next step for Ms. Katrina is to plan a variety of guidance methods to help Perry learn and practice appropriate topic maintenance. Ms. Katrina decides to collaborate with a fellow teacher in order to brainstorm a wide range of possible ways to help Perry learn new ways of interacting during the natural contexts of free play and snack time. She describes Perry's behavior to her colleague. Then, they come up with a host of possible incidental teaching strategies, including the following:

1. Encourage Perry to attend to and try to figure out the themes of play that are emerging. Possible questions include, "Perry, what are they playing about?" "What are they trying to do?" "Who is Sue pretending to be?"
2. If Perry seems to need more than the encouragements described above, offer her some interpretations, such as, "I think they're playing hospital"; "They're bandaging a baby who fell out of its stroller"; "I think Sue is the worried mama."
3. If Perry responds in conversation with a change of topic, redirect her by repeating what her peers said (or asking a peer to repeat), or by paraphrasing what her peer said, or by elaborating on what a peer said. Then prompt her to reply, by saying something like, "Do you have anything to say about that?" or by suggesting to her a specific response. For example, in the broccoli-talk situation, the teacher may follow Perry's escalator comment with, "Tim said,

'broccoli is my favorite,'" or "Carol said she likes to eat broccoli, even though she doesn't like the way it smells," or, "Vinnie's dad makes it with cheese sauce. There are a lot of ways to eat broccoli. How do you like it, Perry?"

4. Gently point out to Perry the apparent unrelated nature of her response; for example, "Carol was talking about eating broccoli. Did that remind you of escalators?" (Well . . . maybe it did. Perry may have an interesting connection to share.) "We're interested to know what *you* think about broccoli, Perry."

At this point, Ms. Katrina has identified Perry as a child who can benefit from incidental teaching, has targeted an area of social competence to work on, has identified potentially fruitful everyday situations during which to be prepared to implement incidental teaching, and has identified a variety of potential incidental teaching strategies to use. With regard to the cycle of reflective teaching, she has identified a general dilemma and defined a problem, and has created a plan of action. It is important to point out here that the list of strategies Ms. Katrina and her colleague developed together is not exhaustive and is not intended to serve as a recipe. By thinking in advance about a myriad of potential incidental teaching strategies, Ms. Katrina has "primed her pump" to be better prepared to respond to whatever the children, and particularly Perry, present. She has some good ideas at the ready, and having done this advance thinking will better enable her to think on the spot and teach appropriately within the moment. This is a valuable characteristic of true reflective teaching.

Ms. Katrina's next step is to implement her plan, observe its apparent impact, and make judgments about its success. Again, the implementation of an incidental teaching plan is not slavish adherence to a prescribed set of steps. Ms. Katrina strives to be available to observe and guide Perry during snack time and the first 10 minutes of free play every day, but this is not always possible. Over the course of 3 weeks, Ms. Katrina's mental list of possible ways to intervene grows and changes as she gains experience with Perry. She occasionally grabs the opportunity to support Perry in situations other than snack time and free play when the occasion presents itself and the time is available. As she implements her plan, Ms. Katrina simultaneously observes the behavior of Perry and her peers, and keeps records of conversational exchanges (in relation to her own intervention tactics) over the 3 weeks. She is careful to note changes in peers' reactions to and behaviors toward Perry, recording anecdotal evidence of the function of "natural reinforcement." A great advantage of incidental teaching is that, as the child's peer interactions improve, the child's behavior is naturally reinforced by the improved nature of her interactions with others and the greater success and inclusion that she experiences. Since this reinforcement is a natural consequence of her behavior, and since it occurs within the natural context of peer interaction, there is little concern about the transfer and maintenance of the newly acquired social skills. In a sense, the child becomes "entrapped" in a cycle of escalating natural reinforcement for increasingly skilled social behavior.

Continuum of On-the-Spot Teaching Strategies

One of the most important means by which teachers can help children learn to interact effectively with one another is to provide on-the-spot support for children when they are in the midst of experiencing a difficult or challenging interaction (Hazen, Black, & Fleming-Johnson, 1984; Katz & McClellan, 1997). Whether the teacher's intervention grows out of an articulated plan for incidental teaching, or whether her intervention is an impromptu act, the degree of support the teacher provides can vary along a wide continuum. A teacher's support during on-the-spot teaching can be thought of as scaffolding. Scaffolding can be defined as the process of providing and then gradually removing external support for children's learning as they are able to take more responsibility for performing an objective (Bodrova & Leong, 1996). A scaffolding approach allows the teacher to support a child's social interaction within that child's "zone of proximal development" (ZPD). The ZPD is "the distance between the actual developmental level as determined by independent problem-solving and the level of potential development as determined through problem-solving under adult guidance or in collaboration with more capable peers" (Vygotsky, 1978, p. 86). The appropriate amount of support for an individual child, then, can be thought of as the least support with which the child can navigate a particular interaction successfully. Appropriate support serves to "build bridges" from the child's current level of ability to new levels of ability (Rogoff, 1990).

Consider the following situation: Two children are playing with shaving cream, spreading it in a thin layer on the smooth tabletop, then scraping it "snow-plow" style with wide tongue depressor sticks. Lee, barely 3, has stood hesitantly a couple of feet away for several minutes watching intently but not speaking. It appears he wants to join in. As his teacher, how might you respond in this situation? Would you stand by without intervening? Would you say to the two players, "Look at Lee standing there"? Would you add, "I think he may want to play with you"? Would you say to Lee, "Do you want to play? What could you do if you want to play?" Would you instead say to Lee, "Go pick up a popsicle stick and you can play at this end of the table?" Would you physically step in, hand

Lee a stick, guide him by the shoulders, and say to the other two, "You work here, Angel, Kay can work at this end, and Lee, you work at this end"? Any of these approaches might be appropriate depending on the needs and capabilities of the particular children involved, as well as on further details of the situation. If this is an uncommon problem for Lee, and you have the time, you may just stand by and see what happens. If this is a common dilemma for Lee, and you have previously attempted less directive approaches, you might step in and model an entry bid for Lee. If the two children at the end of the table have a habit of playing exclusively and ignoring others, you might want to alert *them* to Lee's presence and encourage them to think about what he might want. If you hear a conflict mounting on the other side of the room, you might want to be very directive and get Lee quickly situated with a stick and table space, and move quickly to the block corner.

Observational research conducted in preschool and kindergarten classrooms suggests that unfortunately teachers' actual facilitation of children's naturally occurring peer interaction is often not individualized in relation to the child's age or ability. It has been found that teachers are far more likely to use highly directive or controlling strategies (File, 1994; Kemple, David, & Hysmith, 1997), rather than tuning their support and intervention to individual needs. The continuum shown in Figure 4.1 may help teachers consider and select from a range of on- the-spot teaching strategies to meet individual and situational needs.

Let us begin on the far left of the continuum with the least directive strategy. In some instances, a teacher's proximal *attentive presence* may be

Figure 4.1. Continuum of On-the-Spot Teaching Bevhaviors

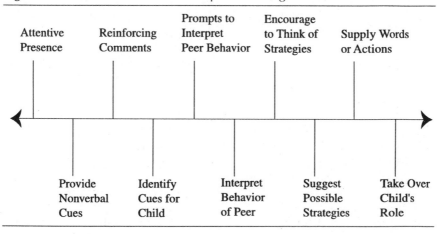

adequate support to allow a child to successfully interact in a challenging situation. Just knowing that an adult is nearby, available to help, and available to protect, may alleviate anxiety and relieve tension enough to allow a child to use his or her social knowledge and skills effectively. A slightly more active and direct role for the teacher is to *provide nonverbal cues* (a look of expectant encouragement, a gentle hand on the shoulder), or *reinforcing comments* such as, "You two look like you're having fun together," or "you worked hard to solve that problem."

The teacher can *identify cues* for the child, helping him or her understand a peer's behavior: "Look at Sally's face" or "Sam's castle is fancy—he is using a lot of blocks" may be sufficient to prompt a peer's helpful behavior toward Sally or cooperation and sharing with Sam. The teacher can provide *prompts to interpret behavior* of a peer: "Let's watch . . . what do you think Janelle is pretending?" may be the amount of support Casey needs to join into Janelle's play. At a higher level of support, the teacher may *interpret behavior* for Casey: "Let's watch . . . I think Janelle is pretending about the three bears." Another example of a teacher interpreting one peer's behavior for another could be, "I think Davis is embarrassed and angry because you laughed when he tripped," which might be sufficient to prompt a show of support toward Davis.

At the next higher level of support the teacher might *encourage a child to think of strategies* to use: "You two both want to work with the drawing program on the computer . . . what could you do about this?" or "How could you let Brittany know that your feelings are hurt?" or "What could you do, to find someone to play Yahtzee with you?" The most direct levels of support on this continuum involve modeling by the teacher. A teacher may model by *suggesting examples of possible strategies*: "Perhaps you could say, 'I will be the cashier' or 'What can I be at the store?' or 'You could tell Mariah 'I am using it. You can have a turn next.'" A slightly more direct strategy would be to *supply the child with words or actions and direct him to use them*: "Go sit down next to Micah and say, 'I want some parquetry blocks too, please' or 'put the game on Hannah's wheelchair tray so you can both reach it.'" At the most directive level of support, the teacher may need to *take over the child's role*. In the example above, she might arrange the game on the tray and demonstrate how to play together. Other examples include: "Martin wants to join your kickball game" or "Terrance, give some Legos to Tim so he can build too" or "Will you play blocks with Sue?", said while modeling for Sue how to point to the photo of blocks on CeCe's communication board.

A similar framework for supporting children's peer interactions in the natural environment has been described by File (1993). File has suggested that, in order to decide upon an appropriate level of support for a specific situation, teachers should ask themselves the following questions:

1. What have I seen this child do before in situations similar to this one? Addressing this question can help teachers focus in on the abilities and developing skills of individuals.
2. How much, or how little, of my help is required for the child to be "successful" in meeting his or her goals in this situation, as well as the goals I have for the classroom? Framing the question in this manner can encourage the teacher to think in terms of what level of support is necessary, but would not take responsibility away from the child that he or she is capable of assuming.
3. How can I keep the children focused on each other rather than on me? Thinking in this manner can help to prevent high levels of intrusion by the teacher. Children can continue to interact with each other to the extent that the responsibility for interactions remains with them rather than being appropriated by the teacher. This question further emphasizes the need to provide only the minimal amount of support required by the child (p. 357).

Further Examples of On-the-Spot Teaching

The following contextualized examples are provided to illustrate various uses of on-the-spot teaching. As you read these, consider whether they are similar to on-the-spot support you have observed or provided. It may also be helpful, as you consider your own examples, to reflect upon whether and how the three guiding questions (described above) have influenced your behavior as you have provided on-the-spot support.

Interpreting Intentions. Dara is playing alone on the playground, riding a tricycle with a cargo wagon attached. She shouts to herself, "Time to head for the hills." Celia hears this, and says she wants to go, too. Dara frowns and says no. Celia reiterates, "But I want to go to the hills, too" and is again turned down. Celia steps to the edge of the trike path and declares, "Well, I'll wait for the next wagon train to the hills." Dara looks puzzled. The teacher steps in and says, "Dara, you have a plan to head for the hills. Celia said, 'I'll wait for the next wagon train to the hills.' Celia is telling you she'd like to play that, too. She wants to ride with you. That way, you can play together." Dara is pleased to hear this. She had not recognized Celia's cues as a bid to play together; perhaps she thought Celia was trying to take her tricycle. The teacher has served to point out and interpret Celia's cues for Dara, helping her to recognize a friendly overture.

Catch Them Being "Good." Yusef and Jill are doing assigned work at the math manipulatives center, creating A-B-B-C patterns. After creating a pattern with unifix cubes, Jill gets a tub of colored beads from the shelf. She trips, which sends beads scattering across the table and onto the floor. Yusef, seeing Jill's distressed expression, begins to pick up beads and put them in the tub. Jill joins in. The teacher smiles, puts a hand on Yusef's shoulder, and says, "Yusef, you are helping Jill. I'm happy you are picking up the beads with her. I think Jill feels good to have a kind friend to help her." The teacher has made a plan and has been on the lookout for opportunities to point out and approve small kindnesses displayed by children. She is doing this as a way to increase children's awareness of and enactment of prosocial behaviors. Instead of waiting for a dramatic display of altruistic heroism (not common in most kindergarten classrooms!), she looks for opportunities to acknowledge behaviors such as holding a door for a peer, moving out of the way, offering help to carry a cumbersome object, or listening attentively as a child speaks during show-and-tell. According to her plan, the teacher points out the specific behavior, describes how it pleases her, and briefly explains why it is a desirable behavior.

Helping a Child Recognize How Her Behavior Affects Others. As adults, we take for granted that our behavior has a bearing on how others react to us. Young children, however, are often not aware of the link between what they do and how their peers respond to them. Mr. Talbot has noted that Anika, who has mild mental retardation, seems particularly unaware of the link between her own social behavior and the responses of her peers. She often uses rough and aversive methods in an effort to gain peers' attention, either by shoving them, grabbing, or slapping at them. While this does gain other children's attention, it is not the kind of attention Anika wants and needs. Peers typically respond angrily, pushing her away or stalking off. In addition to teaching Anika more appropriate ways to get peers' attention, Mr. Talbot makes a plan to seize naturally occurring opportunities to explain peers' responses to Anika. When Anika pushes Tyler to get his attention, Tyler says, "Go away," and stomps off. Mr. Talbot explains to Anika in simple terms, "You want to play with Tyler. When you push him, it makes him so angry he does not want to play with you. You pushed him, so now he doesn't want to play with you. Next time you could say his name 'Tyler' and tell him what you want. You could say, 'Let's play blocks.'"

Prompting Attention. A child who has difficulty attending in conversation may benefit from being prompted to make eye contact, or to position himself or herself at a short distance and in an orientation that makes conversation easier, or to listen carefully to his conversation partner. The following example illustrates ways that a teacher could provide support to facilitate all three of these attending skills. In this situation, two children are working together on a partner collage. A teacher is seated at the collage table.

MISSY: Where should I stick this cotton ball, Joan?

TEACHER: Joan, I hear Missy asking you a question. Look at her eyes.

MISSY: Where should I glue this, Joan?

TEACHER: Hmmm . . . she says "where?" Where do you want her to put it, Joanie?

JOAN: (fidgeting with a toy) You could put it there (vaguely points from a distance).

TEACHER: Move closer to Missy so you can show her. Missy, look at her.

MISSY: (looking into Joan's eyes) Where should I put it?

JOAN: (touching a place on collage) Glue it right on here, Missy. That'll be nice.

TEACHER: You're working together.

Supporting Continuity in Conversation. The ability to establish and maintain a topic of conversation also involves multiple competencies. To establish and maintain a topic, a child must be able to:

1. Recognize the subject being discussed
2. Add information to the subject with comments
3. Get information about the subject by asking questions
4. Answer questions
5. Stay on the subject
6. Take turns and participate in the dialog

The following example illustrates a teacher's facilitation of topic maintenance and topic establishment in an interaction involving two children. They are talking about a tent-like structure that Wes has constructed:

WES: It's a balloon.

TEACHER: A balloon! Wes says he made a balloon.

WES: Hot air balloon. This is where the people go.

TEACHER: Jay, listen to Wes. He's telling you about the balloon.

WES: They ride here.

JAY: What about that?

TEACHER: Jay is curious about that part.

WES: That's not anything. Just the blanket. But this part has the parachutes.

JAY: Batman to the rescue!

TEACHER: (to Jay) Hmm. . . Wes is saying something about parachutes.

JAY: I know. We can put the batmobile on the rope here.
TEACHER: Oh. Tell Wes about it. See what he says.

In this example, the teacher has employed a couple of incidental teaching skills. She has reinforced the subject ("A balloon! Wes says he made a balloon." "Hmmm. . . . Wes is saying something about parachutes.") and she has called attention to children's comments ("Jay, listen to Wes. He's telling you about the balloon."). As the interaction continues, she may also expand the topic and encourage participation by asking questions ("What happens if there is not enough room in the basket for everyone to ride?"). Further excellent examples of such teacher facilitation of peer interaction in the natural context can be found in the video series "Good Talking with You" (Educational Productions, 1987a, 1987b).

CONFLICT MEDIATION

A special case of naturalistic teaching is the process of scaffolding young children's budding ability to resolve conflict through discussion. Considerable attention has been devoted to the role the teacher can play as a mediator who supports children through the process of resolving conflicts that occur naturally in the classroom (cf., Bernat, 1993; Carlsson-Paige & Levin, 1992a, 1992b; Dinwiddie, 1994; Edwards, 1992; Oken-Wright, 1992). While the process may take some time to learn and feel comfortable using, with practice it can become second nature for a teacher: The typical early childhood classroom has no shortage of opportunities to practice conflict mediation!

A Preschool Example

Consider the following preschool example:

Sierra and Artin are in the block area. Artin has been using a dump truck to collect blocks for the skyscraper he is constructing. He leaves the dump truck as he scoots over to the shelf to get more blocks. Sierra notices the dump truck on the floor, and begins to drive it around. When Artin sees this, he dashes over to Sierra and grabs the truck. A tug-of-war begins, and soon both children are angry, shouting, and in tears. This is when the teacher arrives.

How might she respond to this situation? "Sierra, you need to give it back to Artin and say you're sorry" might solve the problem for the moment, but would not help the children learn how to cope with a similar situation in the future. "You two need to work this out" might be an adequate prompt for children who are already skilled in the process of social problem-solving, just as "You need to use your words" would likely only work for children who already know which words to use and how to use them!

With the goal of helping Artin and Sierra eventually learn to resolve conflict independently, the teacher could guide them through the process of resolving their dispute as follows:

1. The children are guided in defining the problem, by allowing each to state his or her perspective on the situation.
2. The teacher helps to ensure that the children understand each other by paraphrasing each child's view to the other and by defining the problem in mutual terms.
3. The teacher lets the children know that they have some responsibility for finding a mutually acceptable solution.
4. The teacher guides them through the process of generating alternative solutions, offering her own ideas when needed, and facilitating children's discussion of the merits of suggested solutions until one is mutually agreed upon.
5. When a solution is agreed upon, the teacher acknowledges the emotional investment each child had in the conflict and the effort that went into finding a solution (cf., Carlsson-Paige & Levin, 1992b; Oken-Wright, 1992).

An illustration of the application of these steps to Sierra and Artin's situation is presented in Figure 4.2.

A Primary Grade Example

The previous example involved dispute over possession of an object, a very common type of conflict among preschool children. The example in Figure 4.3 involves a dispute over conflicting ideas and involves older children:

Clare, Erin, and Kevin have been assigned to work together on an animal habitat mural. The mural will be prominently displayed on the bulletin board outside their second grade classroom, and each of the three feels highly invested in the project's outcome. The children have been working on the mural for a couple of days. They have reached an apparent impasse regarding how to represent the water of a tide pool, such that the animals in the tide pool can be seen. Kevin wants to use a watery wash of

Figure 4.2. Conflict Mediation Illustration: Preschool

Script	Description of mediation
TEACHER: It looks like there is a problem here, Artin and Sierra. You're both pulling on the truck. I'll put the truck on the shelf while we talk about it. What is the problem?	*Neutralize the object of dispute (by removing it).* *Define the problem.*
ARTIN: She stole my dump truck. I need it. SIERRA: I was playing with it.	*Let each child state his or her perspective.*
TEACHER: Sierra says she was playing with the truck, and Artin says he was using it and Sierra took it. You do have a problem. Both of you want the truck. Artin says he had it and Sierra says she had it. And there is only one dump truck available because Dustin is busy with the other one. You need to solve this problem so no one gets hurt and so you are both happy. How could you solve this problem?	*Sum up the problem, defining it in mutual terms.* *Let children know that a mutually acceptable solution must be found.* *Ask for children's ideas.*
SIERRA: Let me play with it.	
TEACHER: Sierra says you could solve the problem by letting her have the truck. What do you think, Artin?	*Paraphrase children's ideas.* *Ask what children think about each other's ideas.*
ARTIN: No! I had it! I want it.	
TEACHER: . . . and Artin says he had the truck and he wants it, Sierra.	
SIERRA: Well, I had it.	
TEACHER: You need to find a solution that is OK with both of you. (Children pout and are silent)	
TEACHER: Hmmmm. What could you do? Sometimes children decide to share. . . .	*Facilitate children's discussion of ideas until one is agreed upon.*
SIERRA: Yeah, we could share.	
TEACHER: How would you do that? How could you share?	
SIERRA: (shrugs)	
TEACHER: Sometimes children share by taking turns.	*Teacher makes suggestions when it seems necessary.*

Figure 4.2. (*continued*)

SIERRA: I could have it for today and he could play with it next week.

TEACHER: Hmmmm. That's Sierra's idea. What do you think about Sierra's idea?

ARTIN: No. I can go first, because I had it and I need it.

TEACHER: Well. You both want to take turns, but you both want to go first. This is still a problem.

SIERRA: Well, I want it.

TEACHER: If Artin goes first, Sierra, what could you do until it is your turn?

ARTIN: The bulldozer! She can have that.

SIERRA: No, the fire truck.

TEACHER: OK, now how about if Artin uses the dump truck for 5 minutes while Sierra uses the fire truck? Then you can switch. Does that sound OK to you, Sierra?

SIERRA: OK . . .

TEACHER: . . . and is that OK with you, Artin?

ARTIN: Yeah, OK.

TEACHER: That sounds like a solution. Artin will use the dump truck while Sierra uses the fire truck, and in 5 minutes you can switch. Let's see how it works out.

When children have agreed on a solution, repeat the solution for them so it is very clear.

TEACHER: (As children begin to play) You were both pretty angry at first. You worked hard to talk about your problem and figure out a solution.

Acknowledge the emotional investment children had in the conflict, and the effort they put into finding a solution.

Observe. If things begin to fall apart, help children discuss it further.

Figure 4.3. Conflict Mediation Illustration: Primary Grade

Script	Description of mediation
MRS. S.: It sounds as if you have a disagreement. Let's move over here to the table and talk about it. What is the problem?	*Define the problem.* *Let each child state his or her perspective.*
KEVIN: I think it will be messy to have cellophane or tissue paper. It will peel and fall down. This needs to look really excellent.	
ERIN: But blue paint won't even look like water. It will change the color of the fish.	
MRS. S.: So, you have different ideas about making the tide pool. Kevin doesn't want cellophane or tissue, because he thinks they will fall off. And Erin doesn't think blue paint will look real. What do you think, Clare?	
CLARE: Tissue paper. Glue it with water. It will . . .	
KEVIN: (interrupting) That will just drip.	
MRS. S.: Let Clare finish, Kevin. You'll have a chance to talk.	
CLARE: It will look like real water.	
MRS. S.: Kevin?	
KEVIN: The glue will drip and be a mess.	
MRS. S.: Well, you do have a problem. Each of you has an interesting idea for making the tide pool. Three very different ideas . . . tissue, cellophane, and paint. You are all making this mural together. You need to find a way to decide how to do the tide pool. Talk to each other. What are your ideas for solving this problem?	*Sum up the problem, defining it in mutual terms.* *Let children know that a mutually acceptable solution must be found.* *Ask for children's ideas.*
ERIN: Cellophane would be shiny like water.	
KEVIN: What about the edges? They'll look bad. This has to be really good.	
MRS. S.: Kevin is really concerned that this look good. What do you think, Clare?	*Paraphrase children's ideas.*
CLARE: Yes. Tape 'em.	
MRS. S.: Tape the edge down? What do you think, Kevin?	*Ask what children think about each other's ideas.*
KEVIN: The tape will look messy. I say, paint.	
CLARE AND ERIN: No!	

Figure 4.3. (*continued*)

MRS. S.: Well, you need to find an idea that you all agree with.

Facilitate children's discussion of ideas until one is agreed upon.

CLARE: Hey, all three.

MRS. S.: All three? Say more about that, Clare.

CLARE: Do all three together.

MRS. S.: Use all three ideas together?

CLARE: Paint, tissue, cellophane. All three.

KEVIN: Oh, brother. We'll be here until Christmas.

ERIN: Hey, I know. We can paint the tide pool with water paint and when it is still wet stick on the tissue. Then put cellophane on top so it's shiny.

KEVIN: What about the edges?

CLARE: (turning to Mrs. S.) Can we staple?

MRS. S.: Can you staple the edges . . . .

CLARE: So it is neat.

MRS. S.: Sure, I can help you staple the edges.

ERIN: (to Kevin) Well?

KEVIN: OK.

MRS. S.: Is it OK with you, Clare and Erin? (the girls nod)

MRS. S.: So, you'll first paint with blue water color, then stick blue tissue on while the paint is still wet. Then staple blue cellophane over that.

When children have agreed on a solution, repeat the solution for them so it is very clear.

KEVIN: Not blue cellophane. It'll be too blue.

ERIN: Yeah, it'll be too dark.

CLARE: Clear cellophane.

ERIN AND KEVIN: Yes.

MRS. S.: OK, clear cellophane. You all had your own ideas that you really liked. At first, it seemed like you'd never decide. But you kept talking to each other and listening to each other, and you found a solution that is OK with everyone. Good work!

Acknowledge the emotional investment children had in the conflict, and the effort they put into finding a solution.

Observe. If things begin to fall apart, help children discuss it further.

pale blue watercolor, painted over the tide pool creatures. Clare wants to glue blue tissue paper, and Erin wants to use blue cellophane instead.

Their teacher, Mrs. Silverman, steps in to help the three children resolve their conflict. She knows that Kevin and Erin are already fairly skilled negotiators, and that Clare, who has above-average intelligence but has a language delay, has not had the same opportunities to practice conflict resolution. In the script provided in Figure 4.3, notice the additional support that Mrs. Silverman provides to Clare by paraphrasing and expanding her utterances and by assuring that her voice is heard. She also provides some special support to Kevin in order to help him recognize and consider others' points of view.

Maximizing Success of Conflict Mediation

Teachers may wonder, "But where would I find the time to do this? And what might happen with the other children while I am attending to these two?" Stein and Kostelnik (1984) found that, during the first 5 weeks of using a conflict mediation process like that described above, the average session lasted 7–10 minutes. That time decreased to a little more than 4 minutes per session by the end of 10 weeks. Extra time invested early in the year can pay off later, as children eventually become skilled in handling their own problems without a teacher's assistance. Teachers often find that, when they are involved in helping two or three children resolve a dispute, other children become interested observers or sideline participants. As a result, problems can be less likely to erupt in other parts of the classroom during this time.

Depending on the needs and abilities of the children involved, the adult can vary the level of support offered through this process: by supplying specific phrases and demonstrating solutions for children who need very direct guidance, or by simply remaining attentive and suggesting, "Think about what to say" for children who can engage in this process fairly independently. For children with limited language, the adult can use very short simple utterances to paraphrase peers' ideas, and take on the child's role when needed. There are certain communication skills that young children do need in order to profit from conflict mediation, including the ability to understand and express such concepts as *if/then, mine, yours, some/all, sad, mad, scared*. Several programs exist that have components designed to help children gain the basic communication skills as a precursor to learning the social problem-solving process (Crary, 1984; Shure, 1992). These programs will be discussed further in Chapter 6.

There are several common mistakes adults make when mediating children's conflicts (Kostelnik et al., 2002):

- *Failing to lay the groundwork.* Conflict mediation will not likely be successful if children are not yet familiar and comfortable with the teacher, the classroom, and the daily routine. Children must have developed a sense of trust in the adult and the environment to profit from the challenging and sometimes long process of conflict mediation. Failing to establish a basic climate of trust, safety, and comfort is likely to undermine attempts to teach conflict resolution.

- *Mandating and masterminding, rather than mediating.* In an effort to expedite the process, adults often err on the side of becoming too directive and controlling in mediating children's conflicts. This denies children the opportunity for the scaffolded practice that helps them to ultimately become responsible for solving their own conflicts. It is best not to begin the mediation process if the adult does not feel that he or she has 5 minutes available to stick with it. Children will not be committed to engaging in conflict resolution in the future if they have had repeated experiences in which an adult has coerced or dictated a solution. In cases when the teacher does not feel that the time is available to legitimately *mediate* a conflict, simple and quick redirection ("Here, Shawna, you use this doll. Let Nadia have that one") may be a better choice.

- *Taking sides.* To effectively serve as a credible mediator, the adult must be perceived by the children as impartial. Each child should have the initial opportunity to state his or her perspective without prejudice or censure from the adult. Nonverbal cues from the adult, such as nodding, frowning, or drumming fingers, and verbal indications of agreement, impatience, or disdain should be avoided. Children must feel confident that their perspective will be heard and given due note (no matter how silly, ludicrous, or wrong that perspective may seem to the adult).

- *Denying children's legitimate claims.* On the other hand, sometimes it is very clear that one child has rightful possession of an object that another child has taken or attempted to take. In such cases, insisting on a compromised solution may deny the child's right to the object. In such cases, the focus should be on helping the "perpetrator" to find acceptable ways to request the object by asking, trading, or bargaining, and to support the possessor's right to say no.

There are several important competencies that children develop as they have repeated opportunities to practice adult-supported social problem-solving. These are not skills that children are likely to learn in a day or a week or a month. Young children need many opportunities to practice resolving real-life disputes, with the support of a skilled and patient adult. Through this process, children can learn to:

1. Define a problem or conflict as a shared dilemma, where there are two points of view
2. Come up with possible solutions to the problem, and choose one to try that takes into account the two points of view and that both children can agree to
3. Put their solution into action
4. Evaluate how their solution worked
5. Predict the consequences of possible solutions prior to implementation

(Dinwiddie, 1994)

At first, most children need a great deal of adult support to move all the way to a negotiated resolution. As children learn the basic competencies of social problem solving, they gradually become more and more capable of resolving conflicts themselves. There is evidence that these competencies developed in childhood are carried forward into adulthood (Goleman, 1995).

While conflict resolution skills are often taught as an alternative to verbal or physical aggressive responses, they are also very important skills for children who are rarely or never aggressive. Learning skills of constructive conflict resolution may be especially important for those children who avoid conflict, who "give in," and/or who push down and swallow their frustration and resentment. Learning the skills of conflict resolution may avert repressed anger, avoid violent response, and enhance creative and innovative thinking.

SUMMARY

On-the-spot teaching and conflict mediation occur in response to spontaneously arising situations in the natural milieu of classroom life. While these strategies may be used effectively on the spur of the moment, they are often the result of careful forethought and practice. Teachers may planfully identify behaviors to target, situations in which to observe for those behaviors, and incidental strategies to implement as the opportunity presents itself. This process may be enriched by professional collaboration. A speech and language therapist, for example, may be a good source of information about on-the-spot teaching strategies to support children's peer communications. The classroom teacher may be a good source of information about the social dynamics of her classroom group and the individual needs and preferences of particular children. For example, the classroom teacher would likely have the greatest information to answer File's (1993) first two guiding questions: "What have I seen this child do before . . . ? How much [support] is required . . . ?" (p. 357). For such a collaboration to work well, the classroom teacher and therapist must be able to "release" their own professional knowledge and be willing to share information and skills with one another. Willingness and ability to share the wealth of one's own expertise and accept being taught the skills and knowledge of another professional's area of expertise is sometimes referred to as "role release." A good source of information about role release and other collaborative skills is the work of Thomas, Correa, and Morsink (2001).

Similarly, the process of helping children learn to identify sources of conflict, generate potential plans of action, put them into action, and evaluate their results takes practice. Though this process is implemented in response to conflicts as they emerge, it requires that the adults know what they want the children to learn, how they plan to help them learn it, and how to adapt to the unique demands of the situation and "think on their feet." On-the-spot teaching and conflict mediation strategies require informed reflection.

FOOD FOR THOUGHT

1. Think back to the principles of environmental arrangement described in Chapter 3. How does "setting the stage" through creation of a physical, temporal, and emotional backdrop help to provide a foundation for the naturalistic interventions introduced in this chapter? In what ways would the naturalistic interventions introduced above be more difficult (or even impossible) to carry out in an inadequately prepared environment?

2. Consider the two scenarios below. As the teacher in each of these situations, what might you do immediately? What might you plan to do later? What additional information would you wish to have to make decisions about intervention? How could you gain that information?
   a. Several children are playing together in the dramatic play area of their preschool classroom. Clarice is assigning roles to others in her usual bossy manner, telling them what to do. She assigns Ruthie to be the "ugly witch." Ruthie protests, and says she wants to be the

princess. Clarice strongly asserts, "I have to be the princess because I am in charge, and I'm more prettier than you. You can be the witch, or you can be the baby." Ruthie stamps her foot, and declares, "I don't like to be a baby or a witch." Clarice says, "Well, you can't play with us, then." Ruthie collapses on the floor in a dramatic display of frustration. (As the teacher, you have observed this entire sequence.)

b. Kindergartners Hector and Carlos are playing together in the fort on the playground, pretending to be Pokémon creatures. Tomas (who has Down's syndrome) approaches the fort and starts to enter. Hector says, "We're not going to play with you, are we, Carlos?" Carlos says, "No. Get out of our fort. No dumb-heads allowed." Tomas runs to you, and says in an agitated and distressed voice, "He said dumb." (As the teacher, you did not observe the interaction.) As you walk with Tomas back to the fort, Carlos runs out and says, in a defensive voice, "Me and Hector want to play alone. Tomas doesn't know how to play Pokémon. He's a baby."

c. A group of second graders have organized a game of kickball on the playground. Leigh Anne approaches you and says, "They won't let Ramsey play because they said he's too slow. That's mean."

Planned Routine Activities to Promote Peer Interaction and Social Inclusion

C HAPTER 4 DESCRIBED naturalistic strategies that teachers use in response to children's spontaneously occurring social behaviors and spontaneously occurring opportunities for social interaction. Teachers plan for on-the-spot teaching such that they are alert to observe for particular situations in which to intervene, and have considered in advance those interventions and support strategies that may be helpful. Chapter 5 describes the use of typical planned classroom activities as natural avenues for supporting children's peer skills and relationships. These strategies are slightly more structured than on-the-spot teaching approaches in that the adult plans and implements an activity for the purpose of (at least in part) creating an opportunity to support peer interaction and/or social cognition.

As is true for any form of activity planning, a teacher begins with particular objectives in mind. These objectives are derived from the teacher's knowledge of important goals of early education, and her knowledge and observation of the particular children with whom she works. Activities are then planned to optimize the likelihood of achieving those objectives. Selection, design, or modification of activities to meet the identified objectives can be enhanced by working together with other professionals who may have more detailed knowledge of, for example, children's literature (a librarian or child psychologist), children's songs (a music teacher or librarian), and activities derived from special education practices, such as PALS centers and group friendship activities (for example, a special education teacher, a guidance counselor, or a teacher specifically prepared for inclusion practices).

SMALL GROUP ACTIVITIES

Cooperative Learning

Cooperative learning is defined as "students working together in groups small enough that everyone can participate in a collective task that has been clearly defined, without constant direct supervision by the teacher" (Cohen, 1994, p. 3). Cooperative learning activities for early childhood can be as diverse as creating a dramatic skit, solving math story problems, planning a meal, writing a story, creating a group collage, compiling a book of information about spiders, cooperating in blowing and popping bubbles or filling and dumping buckets, and writing new words to a familiar song. The defining characteristic of cooperative learning is positive interdependence: Students recognize that they are all working toward a common purpose, that they are all in this together.

True cooperative learning is characterized by the following expectations (Johnson & Johnson, 1991; Kostelnik et al., 2002):

1. All members of a cooperative group are responsible for their own learning and the learning of their group members.
2. Children contribute to one another's learning by helping, supporting, encouraging, critiquing, motivating, and praising each other's work.
3. Each individual is accountable for the group effort. Activities are structured so that each person shares responsibility for the achievement of his or her objectives.
4. Feedback is provided to individuals and the group as a whole. Children have opportunities to reflect on their group work.

Obviously, young children are not developmentally equipped to function in cooperative groups independently. It is up to the teacher to structure the activity and intentionally plan ways for children to learn to work together toward a mutual goal. (For specific suggestions on how to help young children learn to work in groups, see Wasserman, 2000, Chapter 5.) Very young and/or inexperienced children will probably need close adult supervision, with lots of on-the-spot and "just-in-time" support. Older and more experienced children may need little facilitation beyond initial explanation of the activity and the teacher's expectations, as in the following example.

Ms. Awartani has assigned Matt, Kavitha, and Jordan to the task of planning a single day's worth of breakfast, lunch, and dinner menus. The cognitive purpose of the activity is for these 7-year-olds to apply what they have learned about the food pyramid to the creation of a nutritious and balanced one-day menu. In addition, she has identified a specific social skill, "turn-taking," which she has operationalized as (a) one person talking at a time and (b) each person in the group contributing ideas. Turn-taking is a particular area of need for Jordan, who often interrupts and monopolizes conversation. Ms. Awartani explains the academic and social goals of the activity, and specifies her expectations for the children's behavior. She assigns a specific role to each child, and provides a badge for each child to wear with the role labeled and depicted. Matt will be the "recorder" who writes the group's ideas. Kavitha will be the "checker" who makes sure the group is attending to the food pyramid chart present at the table. Jordan will be the "encourager" whose job is to make sure that everyone contributes ideas (this may help him curb his tendency to monopolize). Ms. Awartani will be circulating around the room as the children engage in this activity during center time, but plans to pay special attention to this group and to use incidental teaching strategies to facilitate verbal turn-taking. She is particularly primed to offer verbal praise as she observes the children contributing ideas and attending to one another's ideas, and speaking one at a time. After the activity is completed, Ms. Awartani briefly reviews her expectations for the activity, and asks the children to self-evaluate whether they met the objectives. Did they take turns in sharing ideas? Did each do their job? Did they create a healthy meal plan?

When modified to be developmentally appropriate, cooperative learning activities can be used with very young children. For example, Mrs. Martinez plans a cooperative learning activity to help 3-year-old Molly, who has developmental delay, practice turn-taking skills. For this activity, Mrs. Martinez has analyzed and operationalized turn-taking as being comprised of (1) engaging in a reciprocal behavioral role in cooperation with a peer while (2) waiting for a turn to enact that other child's behavioral role.

Mrs. Martinez chooses patient and cooperative 2-year-old Maddie as a partner for Molly. She explains to the girls that they will take turns being the bubble blower and the bubble popper. While one child blows bubbles, the other will pop them. Then, after a few minutes, they will trade jobs. Mrs. Martinez tells Molly that she will be the first blower and gives her the bubble tumbler and wand to hold. She provides Maddie with a "popper bracelet" to wear, which helps make the popper role more identifiable (. . . when you are holding the wand, you are the blower . . . when you are wearing the bracelet, you are the popper). Mrs. Martinez remains close by to prompt the girls to do their jobs and to prompt switching of roles. She uses "information talk" (sometimes called "broadcasting") to describe what each girl is doing, as a means of encouraging and highlighting the fact that they are enacting their reciprocal roles. "Maddie blows bubbles. Lots of bubbles in the air." "Molly claps her hands to pop those bubbles. Pop pop pop." "Maddie makes bubbles for Molly to pop." When the girls' interest begins to wane, Mrs. Martinez encourages the girls to engage in very simple reflection. She asks the girls, "When you wore the popper bracelet, did you pop bubbles?" "Did you make bubbles with the wand?" "Did you take turns?" She adds her own review, "You took turns. Maddie made bubbles for Molly to pop! Then Molly made bubbles for Maddie to pop. What fun!"

These descriptions provide only a brief overview of cooperative learning, a topic about which much has been written. Further information about cooperative learning activities can be found in Johnson and Johnson (1991).

PALS Centers

PALS centers share many features of cooperative learning. The primary purpose of a PALS center is to increase social interaction among children with and without social delays and/or other special needs (Chandler, 1998). A PALS Center is a play activity center, available during "free play" or "center choice time," in which four factors are arranged for the purpose of promoting peer interaction:

1. Peer selection is made such that children with social skills difficulties are paired with peers who have greater social competence.
2. Adult behavior is arranged such that the adult provides prompts and reinforcement for social behavior as necessary.

3. The adult equips the center with materials selected to promote social play. Materials are limited in variety and number and are of high value to the children.
4. The adult provides initial activity structure by describing child roles and social goals.

The activity at a PALS center lasts about 5 to 15 minutes and involves two or three children at a time. When children are seated in the PALS center, the teacher introduces the activity (for example, a simple game, making a collaborative collage, or dramatic play with props). The teacher describes or demonstrates how to use the materials if needed, describes the social activity goals of the center, and then asks the children to play together. After introducing the activity, the teacher may leave the center and monitor from a distance. Alternatively, the teacher may remain in the PALS center and use it as a prepared context for incidental teaching, prompting children to interact or redirecting to peers initiations made toward her or him. Children who have adequate social skills but use them infrequently, and children who prefer to interact with adults instead of peers, may benefit most when the adult leaves the center. On the other hand, children with poor play skills, communication difficulties, or who are hesitant to engage with peers might benefit more if the adult remains in the PALS center to facilitate (Chandler, 1998). Research has demonstrated that children show an increased frequency in peer interaction when playing in a PALS center (Chandler & Dahlquist, 1993; Chandler, Fowler, & Lubeck, 1992). Following is an example of use of a PALS center:

Maria is 3 years old and was born with [a] cleft palette, resulting in limited verbal communication skills. She communicates primarily through nonverbal gestures and cues and frequently has trouble successfully interacting with peers. As a result, she is often overlooked. To encourage social interaction between Maria and some of the other children, Ms. Beck has decided to use a PALS intervention at the art center, which is Maria's favorite area. Ms. Beck tapes a very large sheet of slick paper to the art table and provides six sponge brushes and three shallow pie pans of thick tempera paint in primary colors. She invites Maria and two friendly and socially competent children, Hsiu-Wen and Sammy, to the center. She says, "I would like you to work together to do one giant painting. You can cover the whole paper with paint, if you'd like. You can share the paint colors." The children quickly begin painting. Because there are limited materials, they must share. Maria pushes aside the red paint she has been using, points at the pan of blue paint Sammy is using, then holds out her hands and makes a whimpering noise. Sammy does not seem to notice

Maria's behaviors. Ms. Beck intervenes by suggesting to Maria, "You can touch Sammy's arm so he'll know you want to tell him something." Maria does, then points and whimpers again. Ms. Beck says to Sammy, "What do you think Maria is telling you, Sammy?" At Ms. Beck's prompt, Sammy says to Maria, "You can use this other brush." Ms. Beck further suggests, "Can you move the pie pan so you can both reach with your brushes?" Maria inches closer to Sammy, who moves the pie pan between them. "Thanks, Sammy, that's helpful," says Ms. Beck. Hsiu-wen then slides her pan of yellow paint toward Maria, saying, "You can share this, too." When Maria dips her blue sponge brush in the yellow paint, Hsiu-wen notes, "Hey, we can make a lot of colors. Can I reach your red?" Maria giggles with pleasure and slides the red pan toward Hsiu-wen. The three children coordinate their activity to cover the smooth paper with bold blocks and sweeping strokes of primary and secondary colors. The trio continue for some time, and seem very pleased with the final result: a muddy gray-green creation they've agreed to call "the mucky swamp." Ms. Beck offers reinforcement by commenting, "You all worked together to make a really muddy mucky swamp!"

In the example above, Ms. Beck has remained in the center to facilitate interactions involving a child who is nonverbal. In the example that follows, the teacher chooses instead to leave the center after introducing the activity.

Five-year-old Ali rarely speaks to anyone in class, and appears to be very shy. When Mr. Conroy has seen Ali in interaction with her father and older brother, she is quite verbal and appears competent. Around peers and Mr. Conroy, she "clams up" and becomes inhibited. Ali seems especially uncomfortable in situations in which boundaries and expectations are unclear. Mr. Conroy thinks that a series of opportunities to play in a PALS center may provide Ali with a nonthreatening context in which to make connection with some of her peers. He decides to begin with a three-way play situation, and chooses Audrey and Elaine, both socially competent and very nurturant 6-year-olds, as partners for Ali. He equips the PALS center with materials for princess dress-up play, knowing that these hold special appeal for all three of these girls. Materials include silky scarves, jewelry, lengths of gauzy and glittery fabrics, net tutus, crowns, and a full-length mirror. Mr. Conroy instructs the girls that their job is to help each other get dressed for the ball and that in 15 minutes he will return with an instant camera so they can take one another's photographs. As the girls begin to sift through the available materials, Mr. Conroy leaves the center to monitor from a distance. Though Ali remains very quiet during the 15-minute period, she appears to enjoy the attention of the other girls. After Mr. Conroy returns with a camera, Ali smiles broadly when Audrey snaps her picture. In subsequent dramatic play PALS activities during the next week, Ali becomes noticeably more comfortable with Audrey and Elaine, and begins to verbally respond to their initiations. Ultimately, she gains sufficient confidence and comfort to initiate toward the two girls and even suggest play ideas. Within 2 weeks time, Ali has two friends.

Cooperative learning activities and PALS centers provide a structure within which small groups of children have multiple opportunities to practice social skills. Within the context of these activities-in-progress, a reflective teacher can make decisions about whether and when and how to support children's interactions using on-the-spot teaching strategies as described in Chapter 4.

WHOLE GROUP ACTIVITIES

Whole-group time, when all children gather together for a common activity, is an integral part of a high-quality early childhood program. Whole-group time provides the opportunity to see the faces and recognize the presence of each individual in the group. As described in Chapter 3, well-planned and well-implemented group times are an important vehicle for creating a feeling of classroom community and inclusion. Whole-group times for young children often include such activities as sharing of literature, music and movement, simple games, puppet demonstrations, storytelling, and brainstorming and other discussion formats. These activities can supply a natural avenue for encouraging social contact among peers and teaching important social lessons, if group times are thoughtfully planned with social competence objectives in mind.

Literature Sharing

Quality children's literature can serve as a wonderful springboard for discussion of friendship, social skills, social dilemmas, and associated emotions. In recent years, there has been an explosion of children's books addressing social and emotional issues. Some of this is high-quality literature, and some is not. Some quality books are appropriate for large-group sharing, while some are better saved for small-group or one-on-one teacher-child sharing. Some books may more appropriately be shared between parent and child. Teachers have a responsibility for determining the appropriateness of books to be shared with the particular children in their setting. That responsibility includes engaging others who can be helpful with literature selection: parents, librarians, fellow teachers, the school guidance counselor, and college instructors who specialize in children's literature can be partners-in-learning for teachers who seek to increase their familiarity with good literature to use for particular social purposes.

In general, good literature for young children should meet the following criteria:

Clarity of writing style
Interesting characters
Suitable illustrations
Relationship to the children's experiential background
Freedom from stereotypes
Brevity
Teacher appeal

That last criterion should be appreciated by any teacher who has tried to read to children a book that he or she truly loathes . . . if you are not positively engaged with the book, the children won't be, either!

In addition, books that deal with emotion-laden topics such as acceptance, friendship, and social competence can be evaluated against the following criteria:

- Can children identify with the plot, setting, dialog, and characters?
- Does the book use correct terminology and psychologically sound explanations, and does it portray events accurately?
- Are the origins of emotional reactions revealed and inspected?
- Does the book reflect an appreciation for individual differences?
- Are good coping strategies modeled for the child?
- Does the book present crises in an optimistic, surmountable fashion?
(Jalongo, 1983)

An annotated bibliography of literature for young children dealing with social relationships, social competence, inclusion, and diversity is included in Appendix A. For additional bibliographies of children's books that deal with peer relationships and ideas for using literature as a social skills intervention, see Jalongo (1983), Kemple and Hartle (1999), Krogh and Lamme (1985), Lamme and McKinley (1992), and Ramsey (1991). Also of interest, Favazza and Odom (1997) describe a successful kindergarten intervention program that uses books and guided discussion, along with structured play opportunities, to promote young children's positive attitudes toward people with disabilities.

Several common social dilemmas that young children face are illustrated in "Let's Be Enemies" (Udry, 1961). This simple, brief, and clearly presented little story deals with the topic of conflict within friendship. The narrator, a young boy, tells us, "James used to be my friend. But today he is my enemy" (pp. 2–3). He goes on to describe James's behavior: James throws sand, grabs the best digging spoon, always wants to be the boss. Adults can use such literature as a catalyst for interactive book sharing, stopping to ask children, "Has that ever happened to you?" or "I wonder what this boy could do when James takes all the crayons." "What did you do when that happened to you?" "How did that make you feel?" Such literary experiences may serve as a vehicle for discussion of difficult life issues, help children feel a common bond with others who have experienced similar feelings and social challenges, and supply children with the confidence and knowledge of strategies to cope more effectively with difficult situations and relationships.

After books have been carefully *selected*, a plan should be made to thoughtfully *share* them with children. Jalongo (1983) suggests the following four steps as a guide for teachers' preparation to share literature in this way:

- *Plan*. Select a book by studying its content and format. Then, prepare questions based on children's background, the story sequence, and concept development. Be sure to plan different levels of questioning.
- *Motivate*. Design introductory remarks that focus the children's attention, define discussion purposes, relate the story to children's experience, and help children identify with the characters.
- *Present*. Read the book, interjecting prepared questions. Respond to children's comments and expressed concerns.
- *Follow up*. Conclude the discussion as needed, by clarifying information, reviewing concepts, answering remaining questions, recognizing children's contributions, communicating acceptance of children's emotional responses, and evaluating the story and discussion. Further follow-up may consist of extension activities in art, writing, music, and so forth that build upon or reinforce the understandings developed through sharing of literature.

Good children's literature can be used to facilitate social inclusion of children with disabilities. In the past 10 years, there has been a surge of publication of books that address disability. Some of these books focus on disability as a primary subject, while other books simply include characters who happen to have disabilities. The bibliography in Appendix A includes both kinds of books. Further suggestions can be found in Blaska (1996) and Blaska and Lynch (1998). *Somebody Called Me a Retard Today . . . And My Heart Felt Sad* (O'Shaughnessy, 1992) is a simply written and illustrated book that can be effectively used as a catalyst for thought and discussion about empathy, name-calling, hurt feelings, disability, and/or diverse developmental levels. The child-narrator begins, "When somebody called me a 'retard' today . . . I cried. I ran away real fast. I hid in my room." The child's father then reminds her of her special qualities: She has friends, she works hard at school, she helps her parents, she does her very best, and she has feelings just like other kids. The book concludes, "I am not supposed to pay attention when they say 'retard.' I'm just supposed to walk away nicely. But I'll tell you a secret . . . When somebody called me a 'retard' today . . . my heart felt sad."

Using the four steps discussed above as a guide, a teacher might plan to present this book to a group of young children in the following way. Introductory remarks might focus on the front-cover illustration, which depicts a dejected-looking child crying in the bottom right corner, and a group of three children pointing and whispering, noses in the air, in the upper-lefthand corner. Children's attention could be focused by asking such questions as:

- What do you see in this picture?
- Why do you think this child might be crying?
- Do you think this child feels sad? Look at this big tear drop.
- What are these children doing up in this corner?
- I think these three children are talking about her. What do you think?
- What do you think this book might be about?

Further introductory remarks might be planned to follow the first three sentences, "When somebody called me a 'retard' today . . . I cried. I ran away real fast. I hid in my room." For instance, depending on the background knowledge of the children the teacher might plan questions and/or remarks to address the word *retard*. If children in the class have used the word frequently, the teacher might not ask for a definition at this point. If she suspects that the word is unfamiliar to (or misunderstood by) some or all of the children, she might ask the children what they think it might mean, and be ready with a definition such as "it is a word that people sometimes use to call someone a 'dummy.' Like 'dummy,' it is a word that can hurt feelings." "Has anyone ever called you a name that hurt your feelings?" "Has anyone ever called you a dummy? How did you feel?" "Let's read and find out more about this child." The teacher might then pose questions and remarks that help the children identify with this child's qualities, likes, and everyday activities.

Concluding the discussion of this book should be planned with care; the last sentences of the book are honest, realistic, and sad. "I am not supposed to pay attention when they say 'retard.' I'm just supposed to walk away nicely. But I'll tell you a secret . . . when somebody called me a 'retard' today . . . my heart felt sad." Lack of clarification may leave children with a sense of resignation and hopelessness. A concluding discussion might be prompted by such teacher questions and remarks as,

- Why do you think those other children called her a hurtful name?
- I wonder if they would call her 'retard' if they knew her better.
- I wonder if they know how she feels.
- What could help the little girl feel better?
- What would you do if someone called your friend a 'retard'?

Later in the day (or throughout the week), children might be encouraged to write or dictate a story about name-calling, or to draw a picture about how they felt when something unkind was said to them.

A different means by which literature can be used to encourage social interaction and facilitate the development of social skills is as a springboard for guided dramatization. Brown, Althouse, and Anfin (1993) have described the use of simple stories as a foundation for interaction via dramatic play. The story "The Three Billy Goats Gruff," for example, was used to help a child with disabilities become engaged in dramatic play with peers. First, the book was shared with the class, with prompts from the teacher to anticipate and predict what would happen next in this repetitive story. The book was placed in the library for individual and small-group reading. A magnetic board with figures from the story was then placed in the classroom. When the child for whom the intervention was created showed interest, the teacher retold the story, moving the characters on the board as she spoke. The next step was to ask the child to select a peer to help her tell the story, using the magnetic board. (At this point, the activity was moved out of the classroom to accommodate the target child's tendency to become distracted). Then small groups of children (three or four at a time) were encouraged to dramatize the story as the teacher told it, choosing props from the classroom to assist them in acting out the story sequence. Next, the teacher took photographs of the children as they analyzed the story. The teacher and children talked about the photos and put them in sequential order. The teacher then wrote what the children said about each photo, and finally read their version of the story aloud. The props and play were eventually moved to the classroom, into the natural context of the housekeeping corner. Gradually, the teacher's assistance was no longer required.

This approach seems quite promising for children who need extra support to become involved in sociodramatic play. Though the idea of "scripted" play may seem unsavory to some teachers concerned with protecting pretend play as a vehicle for self-expression, imagination, and creativity, it is important to recognize that such play can and should serve other functions as well. Because so much of preschool and kindergarten children's social interaction takes place through the medium of social pretend play, it is imperative to provide individual children with the necessary scaffolding to enable them to *participate in the first place*. Once children are included, they can begin to accrue the additional socioemotional and cognitive-linguistic benefits of this important type of play.

Puppetry

Puppets can function as a medium for fostering group discussion about social problems and potential solutions. Puppets provide an opportunity for children to reflect on social dilemmas while they are outside of the "heat-of-the-moment" of a real social problem. Puppetry can also supply a safe context for children to express ideas and emotions that they might otherwise be reluctant to express. Consider the following example:

Ms. Johnson has observed that many of the children in her classroom of 4- and 5-year-olds are experiencing conflicts over who gets to play with the rubber animals, which she has placed in the block area. The children are especially interested in the lion and the elephant. To help children think about how they can solve such conflicts, she plans an interactive puppet "show" to elicit children's ideas. During large group time, she introduces Harry the Hippo (a puppet on her left hand) and Frieda the Fox (on her right hand). Using the piano bench as a stage, Ms. Johnson enacts a conflict between Frieda and Harry using real props from the block area (blocks and the rubber elephant). Frieda and Harry wind up tugging on the elephant and crying, "It's mine! My turn!" Frieda the Fox then turns slowly and purposefully toward the children and declares, "I think we have a problem." Harry the Hippo turns to the children and adds, "Can you tell us what our problem is?" The chorus of voices from the children reply, "You're fighting" and "You're being mean!" Harry the Hippo guides the children to more clearly identify the root of the problem, probing with, "What are we fighting about?" One child says, "The elephant!"

Frieda asks, "What is our problem about the elephant?" A child replies, "You both want it!" Frieda sums up and extends, saying, "We both want the elephant. But there is only one! Oh, help us out! What can we do to solve this problem?"

Through the puppets, Ms. Johnson can guide the children through the process of generating alternative solutions to a problem, evaluating the merits of suggested solutions, and helping children see the potential of these solutions for dealing with real situations (Kemple & Hartle, 1999). Some teachers make such "problem puppet" experiences a regular part of their large-group times (cf., Kreidler, 1984; Shure, 1992).

Puppetry can also be used as an extension of literature sharing. "Bibliotherapy through puppetry" (Clarke, 1985) involves first sharing a story with children (e.g., books about jealousy, friendship, sharing, quarreling), and reading the book several times over the course of a few days until children are familiar with the story. Then, children can be invited to reenact the story (in their own ways) using puppetry. Finally, the teacher may use careful questioning to guide children's discussion of the story and of their own relevant experiences. Puppets can provide children with a safety shield that enables them to share strongly felt emotions and discuss difficult topics, with a candor and comfort level that might otherwise be absent.

Group Affection Activities

A group of fifteen 3- and 4-year-old children are on the "circle time rug," playing a teacher-facilitated version of Farmer in the Dell. Instead of the usual "The farmer takes a wife . . . the wife takes the child . . . the child takes the nurse . . . ," the children sing and enact the following: "The farmer hugs his wife, the farmer hugs his wife, Hi-ho the Derry-O, the farmer hugs his wife. . . . The wife pats the child, the wife pats the child, Hi-ho the Derry-O, the wife pats the child . . . The child says 'I like you' to the nurse . . . " and so forth.

The term "group affection activity" (also called "group friendship activity") is used in the early childhood special education literature. While the term may be unfamiliar to many general early childhood teachers, the activities themselves are likely to be familiar. Group affection activities have been defined by McEvoy, Twardosz, and Bishop (1990) as typical preschool games, songs, and activities that have been modified to include teacher prompts for varying types of affectionate responses.

Group affection activities allow children with and without disabilities to encounter one another in a gradual and nonthreatening way, through the medium of a pleasant and fun activity. Through group affection activities, children have the opportunity to observe peer models engaging in friendly behaviors and verbalizations, to practice friendly interactive behaviors, and to receive positive teacher attention for doing so. Affection activities have been successfully used to increase the interactions of children who are isolate or withdrawn (Twardosz, Nordquist, Simon, & Botkin, 1983); have autism (McEvoy et al., 1988); have mental retardation (Brown, Ragland, & Fox, 1988); or have been abused or at risk for abuse (Niemeyer & McEvoy, 1990).

Brown and Conroy (1997) provide teachers with the following tips for successful implementation of group affection activities:

- Identify preschool activities, songs, and games in which can be embedded encouragement to interact with peers and teacher acknowledgement of those peer interactions during common preschool activities.
- Before implementation of friendship activities, determine which children (both target children and socially sophisticated peers) will participate; when the friendship activities will be performed; which preschool activities will be employed as the context for facilitating children's peer interactions; and what materials (if any) will be needed to conduct friendship activities.
- Before the initial implementation of friendship activities, prepare participating children by discussing how the group activities will change (i.e., explicit encouragement to socially interact with peers, teacher acknowledgement of peer interactions) and the purpose of the changes (i.e., to become better "friends").
- Before the start of every friendship activity, remind children of the purpose of friendship activities and discuss the importance of positive social interactions and making friends.
- Provide ongoing teacher support by systematically encouraging target children to socially interact with peers who are more socially sophisticated. Acknowledge peer interactions with praise.

Innovative teachers can find ways to transform many preschool games and music/movement activities into group affection activities. A few examples of familiar games and songs modified to include affectionate responses are provided in Figure 5.1. Other sources of ideas for group affection activities are fellow teachers, including, of course, early childhood special education teachers. A 1-hour creative brainstorming session among the early childhood staff at your school is likely to result in a good collection of ideas for group affection activities designed to provide practice of a variety

Figure 5.1. Examples of Games and Songs Modified for Use as Group Affection Activities

---

If you're happy and you know it: If you're happy and you know it, clap your hands. . . . If you're happy and you know it, hug a friend. . . . If you're happy and you know it, smile at a friend. . . . If you're happy and you know it, shake hands with your neighbor . . . etc.

Simon says: Simon says, say hello to a friend. . . . Simon says, say something nice to your neighbor. . . . Simon says, hold a friend's hand . . . etc.

Hokey Pokey: You put your right hand in, you put your right hand out, you put your right hand in, and you shake it all about. We play with special friends, so shake your neighbor's hand, that's what it's all about. BEING FRIENDS! . . . We play with special friends, so put your arm around a friend, that's what it's all about. BEING FRIENDS! . . . etc.

---

of friendship behaviors. This could constitute a productive (and enjoyable) staff meeting.

Group affection activities are easy to implement, require little teacher training or advance preparation, and are fun for children. Research has shown that group affection activities can be used successfully to promote social interactions between young children with and without disabilities, and increased interactions generalize to free play settings after implementation of group affection activities (Niemeyer & McEvoy, 1990). However, these activities may be ineffective or insufficient for many children and will probably work best with children who already know how to interact but are not doing so (McEvoy, Odom, & McConnell, 1992). (For further information about using group affection activities, see McEvoy, Twardosz, & Bishop, 1990.)

Music

In Chapter 3, I introduced music as a medium for creating classroom community, shared culture, and a climate of caring. In the group affection activities described above, music is often a key element. Teachers can also use music as a tool to encourage social awareness and competence by selecting and planfully integrating into the curriculum songs that address friendship, acceptance, social awareness, and/or social behavior. Similar to the way that literature can be used as a catalyst, carefully selected songs can be used as a springboard for discussion and can lead to follow-up and extension activities across the curriculum. Music has a special motivating quality, as it readily evokes children's emotional engagement. Songs that are heard and/or sung repeatedly become familiar; their familiarity then makes them an easy foundation upon which to build conversation and other extension experiences. Appendix B lists recorded songs that promote the social goals of acceptance and competence. In addition to music teachers, fellow classroom teachers and parents can also be good sources of children's songs. Some parents have spent many hours engaged in second-hand listening as their young children's favorites play on the tape deck.

Many of the songs listed in Appendix B celebrate friendship in a broad and general way, while some songs target specific prosocial behaviors. For example, "The Sharing Song" (Raffi, Pike, Simpson, & Simpson, 1976) is useful for facilitating discussion of this particular set of social skills whose complexity is often underestimated by adults. The song identifies a variety of entities and quantities that are shared in different ways (cake, blocks, a book), and points out "'Cause if I share it with you, you'll have some too."

Adults often admonish young children to "share" without helping them understand how to do so. Often children come to believe that sharing simply means "you give it to me" or "I give it up." In some situations, several ways of sharing are possible. In other circumstances, some ways of sharing are not feasible. Materials or territory can be shared by taking turns, by simultaneous use (which may be parallel or cooperative), by division, by substitution, or by compromise. "The Sharing Song" mentions three things that are typically shared in very different ways. Food is generally shared by dividing it; blocks are shared by substituting, dividing, or compromising (a single block is typically shared by substitution or compromise); and a book is usually shared by taking turns or by simultaneous cooperative use. Teachers can guide children to consider the various meanings of *share* implied in "The Sharing Song" by soliciting children's suggestions for how cake, a block, or a book could be shared and by prompting children to consider how other objects, materials, and territory could be shared. How could you share the paste? The block area? The easel? A doll? The Legos? Your umbrella? Are some things easier to share than others? Are there some things you should not have to share?

Music can serve a unifying function in an early childhood classroom. Favorite songs, sung together and frequently, contribute to a sense of classroom community and shared culture. Recordings of quiet, calming music played repeatedly during rest time or quiet activities provides a continuity and familiarity that is reassuring to young children. Piggyback-style songs provide an avenue for teachers and children to create their own songs about social topics. For example, piggybacking upon the tune of "Mary had a Little Lamb," a new song could be "Suzy has a friend named Sam, friend named Sam, friend named Sam. Suzy likes her friend named Sam because they both like blocks (. . . because he is so funny . . . because he likes to sing . . .)." Music holds emotional appeal for human beings; as such, it can contribute to a pleasant atmosphere conducive to positive social interaction.

More about Group Discussion

Actual social dilemmas that were experienced by a few children in incidents during the school day can be imported to group time to serve as a catalyst for class discussion. While on-the-spot guidance is invaluable, "post-problem" discussion provides children with an opportunity to calmly examine and evaluate real and personally relevant social dilemmas (and potential solutions) away from the heat and passion of the moment of the problem. Group discussion also allows children to learn from the variety of perspectives offered through collective reflection. For example, a first grade teacher asks her class if anyone would like to describe something fun they did with friends during recess. She then asks, "Did anyone have a problem during recess that they would like to talk about?" One girl volunteers, "They locked me in the dungeon under the jungle gym. I told them I don't want to play boys-chase-girls, but they never listen." The teacher uses questions like, "What did you say to them, to let them know you didn't want to play?" "What could she do, to let them know she doesn't want to play that game?" to guide the discussion, and help children to consider when "no" really means "no," and when it is only part of the pretense. Discussion may lead the group to agree to a signal that means, "I'm not kidding. I really don't want to be chased and captured. I don't want to play." Based on problem-solving discussions generated by puppets, songs, books, actual situations, or hypothetical role play, teachers and children can maintain a booklet or poster-sized list of strategies for dealing with social dilemmas. As children continue to discuss social problems, new ideas can be added to the list. The list can be used as a resource during group discussion, or can be referred to as the teacher steps in to provide on-the-spot assistance with a challenging situation (Kemple & Hartle, 1999).

SUMMARY

Incidental teaching, conflict mediation, cooperative learning, and such group time activities as literature sharing and group affection activities, are among the naturalistic ways that teachers may intervene within the typical activity of early childhood classroom life. These interventions are generally easy to implement, and are in fact so natural that they may best be considered part and parcel of any high-quality early childhood program. The naturalistic interventions discussed in this chapter and in Chapter 4, as well as the environmental arrangements described in Chapter 3, could be considered *necessary* components of a high-quality, inclusive early childhood program. They may, however, not be *sufficient* to promote social competence and inclusion for all children. More intensive interventions, to be described in Chapter 6, may be warranted for some young children.

FOOD FOR THOUGHT

1. Select one of the following social competencies, and describe how you might create a PALS center or cooperative learning activity to promote the development of that competency:

   - Providing assistance to peers
   - Sharing play materials with peers
   - Repeating, expanding, or clarifying a peer's comments
   - Suggesting joint play with a peer
   - Taking turns during play activities
   - Responding to a peer's initiation

   Consider the potential role of incidental teaching strategies, as described in Chapter 4, in supporting this intervention.

2. Select another of the above competencies and describe how you might use large-group time activities to promote the development of that competency. Consider the potential role of incidental teaching strategies, as described in Chapter 4, in supporting this intervention.

3. Describe how you might create a PALS center or cooperative learning activity to promote the development of these additional social competencies:

   - Working together toward a common goal
   - Considering another person's point of view
   - Resolving differences of opinion

   Consider the potential role of incidental teaching strategies, as described in Chapter 4, in supporting this intervention.

4. Describe how you might use large-group time activities to promote the development of all three of those competencies. Consider the potential role of incidental teaching strategies, as described in Chapter 4, in supporting this intervention

CHAPTER 6

High-Intensity Training and Coaching Interventions

THIS CHAPTER DESCRIBES teaching approaches labeled as *high-intensity* coaching and training interventions. These are strategies at the less normalized, less natural end of the spectrum. These highly planned approaches typically involve directly instructing children in social skills and using intentional alteration of social contingencies to influence behavior. They are sometimes initiated in a setting apart from the natural classroom environment and sometimes are carried out entirely within the classroom. High-intensity interventions are typically used for children with very significant difficulties related to social competence, for whom more normalized interventions (like environmental arrangement and on-the-spot teaching) have been deemed insufficient.

Successful implementation of these higher intensity interventions requires both the combined expertise of the general classroom teacher and other professionals who possess knowledge and skills in behavior analysis, prompting, and effective use of reinforcement (such as a special education teacher or behavioral psychologist). Implementation of these strategies will generally grow out of collaboration among a team of professionals. The example below is designed to illustrate how a teacher may initiate collaboration and engage in reflection for the purpose of addressing the social needs of a child entering a classroom mid-year. In this case, the teacher is challenged to intervene quickly, knowing that a more comprehensive plan for intervention will need to be worked out soon after, with the support of colleagues.

INTEGRATING A NEW STUDENT

Five-year-old Javier joined Mrs. Bowen's kindergarten class in January. On his first day, Mrs. Bowen introduced Javier to the group during greeting circle. She invited each child to introduce the child sitting next to him or her and tell something special about that person. She then invited Javier to share something about himself. "I'm the blue power ranger," said Javier in a gruff but quiet voice while lowering his eyes and hunching his shoulders. Mrs. Bowen requested that Damien, a friendly, adaptable, and mature child, be Javier's guide for the day, helping him to learn about being in this kindergarten class. Both boys agreed. Mrs. Bowen made a quick decision to simplify her plans for the day so she could be available to get to know Javier and help him "learn the ropes" as needed. During morning recess, Javier pushed a child off of a swing in order to play on it himself. Mrs. Bowen told Javier to come off the swing and sit by her while she comforted the pushed child. She said gently but firmly to Javier, "You wanted to swing. I'm concerned that you pushed Stephan off the swing. He was having a turn, and now he is hurt. Stephan can get back on the swing. You can play somewhere else, Javier, I will help you find a place. In 5 minutes if you still want a turn we can figure out a way to ask Stephan."

Looking dazed, Javier complied and went to the sand area. Mrs. Bowen followed him there and chatted with Javier about his activities in the sand. After 5 minutes, Mrs. Bowen said, "Would you still like a turn on the swing, Javier?" Javier nodded, and Mrs. Bowen said, "What could you say to Stephan, to get a turn?" "Give it to me," bellowed Javier. "You could say that. I think that might make him mad. You could say, 'Stephan, can I have a turn in 2 more minutes?' Can you say that to me?" Javier rehearsed as requested. "Great," said Mrs. Bowen. Let's go try it. At the swing set, Mrs. Bowen prompted Javier, "Say 'Stephan . . . ' "Stephan, I want a turn. In 2 minutes?" said Javier. "Well, how about 3 minutes?" responded Stephan. Javier nodded OK. Mrs. Bowen checked her watch and waited with a friendly arm around Javier until 2 minutes had passed. "One more minute," she said to Stephan. Ultimately, Javier had his turn on the swing. Mrs. Bowen felt pleased.

Momentarily, Mrs. Bowen noted that Javier had left the swing. He stood by a huddle of boys who were playing something down on the grass. Mrs. Bowen suspected that Javier might want to join them. As she walked over to see if her assistance would be needed, Javier kicked one of the boys, knocking him over, then fled. The morning went downhill from there. By lunchtime, Javier had shoved two more children and had stormed into the manipulatives area as the blue power ranger, knocking over the tubs of Cuisinaire rods and Unifix cubes. At lunchtime, Mrs. Bowen went to the office to get Javier's home phone number. She hoped to contact Javier's parents to be sure she could spend a few minutes with them at the day's end. She felt the need to establish a relationship with these parents as quickly as possible. At the front desk, she learned that Javier would be riding the bus home, so a face-to-face conversation would not likely occur that afternoon. She dialed the phone number, but got no answer. She learned in the office that Javier and his mother had just moved from another state. The local address was one that Mrs. Bowen recognized: A highly transient, run-down apartment complex about 4 miles from the school.

With 90 minutes of the school day remaining, Mrs. Bowen went to retrieve her class from the lunchroom. She was met by an exasperated lunchroom attendant, who informed her that "the new boy" had pushed a girl off the side of the lunch bench, sending her tray of food flying and causing her to hit her elbow hard on the edge of the bench. The girl, Karena, was on her way to the nurse's station. Javier sat banished to a corner of the lunchroom with arms crossed tightly over his chest, shoulders hunched protectively up to his ears, chin to chest, and an angry grimace on his face. Mrs. Bowen stood for a moment and contemplated the angry, lost-looking little boy from a distance. She knew that she'd have a lot of thinking to do after the school bell rang. She recognized that she needed to intervene, she needed to intervene quickly, she needed to intervene in multiple ways, and she needed help. She walked to the corner to take Javier by the hand.

This example illustrates some of the challenges involved in teacher decision making in real-life situations. It would be helpful if Mrs. Bowen had known in advance that Javier would be joining her class. She could have learned something about him, let him know something about her and about the class he would be joining, and could have made plans with his mother about facilitating his transition. Instead, Javier simply showed up at her door one Monday morning at 8 a.m. with an office assistant who announced: "This is Javier Sanchez. He will be in your class." In the real world of public elementary schools (and many private programs as well), this unfortunately is often the way a teacher and a "new child" are introduced. Mrs. Bowen knows virtually nothing about Javier at 8 a.m. By day's end, she has tentatively surmised that he has difficulty sharing, taking turns, and verbally communicating his needs. He uses physically aggressive tactics in an effort to get his needs met. He likes power rangers. He wants to engage other children. He seems angry, defensive, and scared. Mrs. Bowen needs to know more about this little boy.

That evening Mrs. Bowen calls the Sanchez phone number three times but gets no answer. Nonetheless, she knows that she needs to have a plan in place by tomorrow morning: Not a comprehensive plan, not the final plan, but a plan of action to help Javier during the next day, and a plan for how to begin to create a larger intervention plan.

In general, it is suggested that a teacher consider the least intrusive, most normalized forms of support and intervention first. This principle would suggest that Mrs. Bowen consider first environmental factors and how she can arrange these to best support Javier and help him learn to use more appropriate social behavior. If these are deemed insufficient, she may consider the more direct strategies for support and intervention, which were described as "naturalistic interventions" in Chapters 4 and 5. It seems likely that with Javier she may also need to employ more intensive approaches, and we will consider those shortly.

In this situation, Mrs. Bowen is faced with a serious dilemma. It will take time to get to know Javier, observe his behavior with peers, and gain the trust and cooperation of his mother. Mrs. Bowen, however, does not feel that she *has* time: Javier physically hurt five children during his first day at school. Though none was seriously injured, Mrs. Bowen noted that the forcefulness of Javier's aggression increased over the course of the day. She is concerned for the physical and psychological safety of the other children in her class. She knows that if Javier's reputation as an aggressor is allowed to solidify in the next couple of days, it will be difficult to overcome. Once a child has established a reputation as someone to be avoided, behavioral change on the part of the child is often not enough to alter his or her social acceptance in the eyes of the peer group (Hymel, Wagner, & Butler, 1990). Mrs. Bowen also recognizes that there are a couple of children in the class who may be positively "impressed" by physically aggressive behavior. She is concerned that if Javier is allowed to gain instrumental success or power through aggressive behavior, that behavior may be reinforced by the admiration and prestige accorded to him by those susceptible peers. Mrs. Bowen believes she needs to act fast.

In thinking about tomorrow, Mrs. Bowen draws the following conclusions. She needs to begin to establish a relationship of trust with Javier, and needs to learn more about his interests and aptitudes so that she can build upon them. In addition, she thinks that a system of tangible reinforcement may help to curb Javier's aggressive behavior in the short term and enable him to have at least a couple of successful experiences with peers.

Mrs. Bowen picks up the phone at 9 p.m. and calls Ms. Janowitz, the school's behavior specialist. She quickly describes Javier and the day's events, and her own thinking about how to approach tomorrow. Together, they sketch out a plan and agree to meet at 7:15 tomorrow morning to finalize what they will do.

A Plan for Helping Javier

In order to allow Mrs. Bowen the flexibility and time to get to know Javier a little better, Ms. Janowitz will participate in the classroom as a second teacher from 8:00 until 11:00 a.m. Mrs. Bowen will set aside the more demanding and teaching-intensive portions of her lesson plan for the day, and substitute easily managed activities in which the children can engage with little adult support.

Once again, Mrs. Bowen will request that Damien serve as Javier's buddy for the day. In addition, she has planned three special experiences for Damien and Javier to engage in together. They will serve together as table washers after snack time. They will work on creating new signs for the classroom centers, to replace the tattered and worn signs that indicate the number of children allowed in each center. They will serve as co-line leaders (a job that requires gently holding hands). Mrs. Bowen will be close by to supervise and scaffold each of these three simple experiences. She will provide support, encouragement, and praise for prosocial behaviors (helping, cooperating, sharing, kind words) displayed during these experiences.

The main activity for the morning will be creating "all-about-me" books. Mrs. Bowen will present this to the children as an opportunity to add to their classroom library. She will provide an initial purpose for the activity by explaining that it will be a way for each child to let Javier know something about them, and for Javier to let them know about him.

Mrs. Bowen will quickly sketch out several fill-in-the blank pages, such as

My name is _____.
My favorite thing to do at home is _____, because _____.

My favorite thing to do at school is _____, because
_____.
I am really good at _____.
Something that makes me really happy is _____.
Something that makes me really angry is _____.

The kindergarten aide can make copies in the workroom for each child. Sitting one on one with Javier while he works on his all-about-me book will provide Mrs. Bowen a chance to listen, probe, and learn about Javier.

Because most of the morning activities will require minimal adult support, Mrs. Bowen and Ms. Janowitz plan to unobtrusively observe Javier and jot down anecdotal records. They plan to pay particular attention to his efforts to engage peers and his interests. Both teachers will look for opportunities to support, encourage, and praise signs of prosocial behavior by all of the children, with special attention to Javier.

At the beginning of the morning, following greeting circle, Mrs. Bowen will take Javier aside to talk about her reinforcement plan. She will talk with Javier about the class's golden rule: "We take care of each other—no hurting." She will remind him of the previous day's incidents. She will explain to him that she wants to help him have friends to play with and have a good time at school. She will explain the token system. For each 15 minutes that Javier does not hurt a classmate's body (by pushing, hitting, kicking, or other actions that hurt), he will receive a sticker. He can then place the sticker on his own sticker chart (a brightly colored piece of cardboard with his name on it, divided into rows and columns 4 × 4). Each time he earns four stickers, he can choose a reward from a treasure box. The treasure box has been borrowed from Ms. Janowitz's office. It contains a variety of rewards, including small toys and trinkets, and tickets with privileges described on them. The reward choices are diverse, because Mrs. Bowen does not yet know what will be appealing and serve as a reinforcer for Javier. Mrs. Bowen will accompany the award of each sticker and the award from the treasure box with social reinforcement. Social reinforcement will be in the form of praise ("I saw you playing Legos near Stephan. You were sharing the Legos," or "You followed the rule. You took care of people. No one got hurt.") and physical gestures such as a warm smile, a gentle hand on the shoulder, or a friendly hug.

In addition to employing certain classroom strategies, Mrs. Bowen intends first to ask an office assistant to work on getting hold of Mrs. Sanchez (getting a work phone number for her so a meeting can be arranged), and then to meet with Ms. Janowitz at the end of the day to compare notes and collaborate on planning potential next steps.

In sum, Mrs. Bowen's plan for Javier's second day in her class includes strategies of varying types: temporarily altering the ratio of adults to children, structuring a social partnership, incidental teaching, and a planned activity to help children learn about one another. The plans also include a somewhat higher intensity teacher-mediated intervention in the form of a structured system of reinforcement.

INTERVENTION STRATEGIES

The term *teacher-mediated intervention* refers to a variety of approaches, including teacher-led social skills training groups, teacher-provided prompts for social interaction, and teacher-provided reinforcement for social interaction. Often, some combination of the three are implemented together. These are interventions that are highly planned, directed, and monitored by the teacher (Conroy & Brown, 2002). These interventions will generally be developed by a collaborating team of professionals; for example, the classroom teacher, a behavior specialist, a special education teacher, and a speech and language specialist. In the case of a young child with a disability, these interventions may be developed as part of the child's Individual Education Plan (IEP). Teacher-mediated strategies typically involve prompts and reinforcement for social interaction directed by the teacher to the target child or target children to whom the social behaviors are to be taught. Typically, the teacher provides instruction, then uses predetermined verbal statements and physical cues or gestures to prompt a child to use a specific social initiation (for example, offering a toy) or to respond to an initiation by a peer. The interaction that results is then rewarded by the teacher, usually through verbal praise, tangible rewards such as stickers, or a combination of social and tangible rewards.

Prompts

A *prompt* is a verbal or physical cue provided by an adult to a child in order to initiate an interaction or to respond to the initiation of others. For example, Mr. Greene instructs Thom that when he says "Look at your friend" it is a signal to turn toward a child who is speaking to him and look at that friend's face. When a peer initiates toward Thom, Mr. Greene looks at Thom's face and points his hand toward the peer, dramatically turning his eyes and face toward the peer while saying to Thom, "Look at your friend." As Thom consistently responds appropriately by turning and attending to peers, his teacher reduces the verbal prompt to "look," then eventually drops the verbal prompt entirely and uses only the physical gesture. Ultimately, Mr. Greene drops the gesture when the peer's verbal initiation itself becomes a reliable prompt for Thom to turn his face, look at, and attend to an initiating peer.

When adults use prompts to direct children's use of appropriate social behavior, it is important that the prompts be faded so the children do not become dependent upon the prompts and so that the children will come to respond to the natural stimulus without adult prompting. The "system of least prompts" is an effective means of fading adult prompts (Wolery, Ault, & Doyle, 1992). This method involves presenting children with a sequence of prompts that build in degree of intrusiveness (or the degree to which the prompt controls behavior). For example, Ms. Van Sant prompts Peter, who has mental retardation, to respond to peers' requests that he pass the snack plate. Beginning with a minimally controlling prompt, Ms. Van Sant says, "Peter," while gesturing toward the peer who has made the request. Ms. Van Sant allows a few seconds for Peter to respond by passing the plate. If he does not, Ms. Van Sant says, "Pass the plate" and allows time. If Peter still does not respond appropriately after a few seconds, Ms. Van Sant puts the plate in Peter's hands, saying again, "Pass the plate." If Peter still does not perform the behavior after a few seconds, Ms. Van Sant holds the plate with Peter's hands while passing it for him, repeating "Pass the plate." On subsequent occasions, Ms. Van Sant stops the prompting sequence whenever Peter responds appropriately. With continued use, the less intrusive prompts take over the control of responding so that the progression to more intrusive prompts is unnecessary. Eventually, control of responding is transferred to the natural stimulus, in this case the peer request, "Please pass the snack, Peter." Prompting procedures are frequently combined with reinforcement. In this case, when Peter does pass the snack plate, Ms. Van Sant smiles and says, "Good, Peter!" and encourages the peer to say, "Thanks for passing the snack, Peter."

Reinforcement

Frequently, prompting is combined with reinforcement. A large body of research supports the powerful effects of teacher prompting and praise on the social behavior of young children with disabilities (McEvoy, Odom, & McConnell, 1992). *Reinforcement* refers to consequences that increase the likelihood that a particular social behavior will be repeated, and may include praise, tangible reward (e.g., stickers, trinkets, tokens), and/or the opportunity to engage in desirable activities. When using reinforcement as a social skills intervention, research suggests that it is important to wait until a social interaction has completely stopped before administering reinforcement. Then, children's interaction will not be interrupted while turning their attention to the teacher (Peterson, McConnell, Cronin,

Spicuzza, & Odom, 1991; Strain & Fox, 1981). As is the case with prompts, it is important to systematically fade out the use of reinforcement, so that children will not be dependent upon the continuing application.

Positive reinforcement strategies are generally used to teach, maintain, or strengthen behaviors (Zirpoli, 1995). A particular behavior is said to be positively reinforced when the behavior is followed by the presentation of a reward (for example, praise or a sticker) that results in increased frequency of the specified behavior (Schloss & Smith, 1998). A reinforcer is defined in terms of its result: If the targeted behavior increases in frequency, the reward was a reinforcer. If the frequency does not increase, the reward did not serve as a reinforcer. For example, Ms. Kelly begins to consistently praise Ferris for hanging his sweater on his hook, saying words like, "Great, Ferris! You put your sweater on your hook. You will know just where to find it when we go outside." If Ferris hangs his sweater on his hook more consistently, we can say that Ferris's sweater-hanging behavior has been positively reinforced.

The following is an example of a teacher-mediated intervention using prompts and reinforcement:

Rocky, age 5, enjoys engaging with his peers. Rocky has *spina bifida* and for mobility uses a wheelchair equipped with a tray. Often children play near Rocky without recognizing that he would like to play but simply cannot reach the play materials. He rarely requests that they bring him out-of-reach materials. Rocky's teacher, Mr. Ian, has worked individually with Rocky, utilizing explanation, demonstration, and role play to instruct him to use a child's first name followed by a request to bring a desired toy (e.g., "Tameka, please bring me some Legos"). During center time and outdoor play, Mr. Ian prompts Rocky to ask his peers for materials by modeling a short phrase and then rewards his appropriate verbalization by saying, "Good request, Rocky." Mr. Ian begins delaying his prompts because Rocky is now requesting materials appropriately. After the prompts are suspended, Mr. Ian plans to fade the reinforcers by gradually praising the targeted behavior less frequently and less predictably.

Reinforcers that teachers use typically fall into one of three categories: social, activity, and tangible reinforcers. Social reinforcers are typically the most "normalized." They mimic the natural consequences of positive prosocial behavior. Tangible reinforcers are the least normalized in that they involve the introduction of rewards that are not part of the ordinary routine. In selecting a reinforcer, the goal is to select the least intrusive reinforcer that is likely to be effective. It is generally suggested that if activity or tangible reinforcers are warranted, the teacher should have a plan for gradually moving toward social reinforcers. This can generally be accomplished by coupling activity or tangible reinforcers with social reinforcers. Once the desired behavior is firmly established, the tangible or activity reinforcers may be gradually removed while the social reinforcers continue (Duncan, Kemple, & Smith, 2000).

Social Reinforcers. When teachers use interpersonal interactions to effectively reinforce a behavior, they are using "social reinforcers" (Schloss & Smith, 1998). Commonly used social reinforcers include praise, smiles, hugs, a pat on the back, and a light squeeze on the shoulder. Social reinforcers are the most frequently used type of reinforcer in early childhood classrooms, probably because they are convenient, practical, and can be highly effective (Sulzer-Azaroff & Mayer, 1991). The example involving Ferris hanging his sweater illustrates use of social reinforcers.

Activity Reinforcers. Teachers use activity reinforcers when they employ access to desired activities as reinforcement (Sulzer-Azaroff & Mayer, 1991). Commonly used activity reinforcers include doing a special project; being a classroom helper or other desirable privileges; having extra free choice time, extra playground time, or a party; and playing with an intriguing new learning material. A good way to think about selecting an activity reinforcer to use with an individual child is to ask oneself, "If this child had complete freedom to choose what to do in the classroom, what would he or she most often choose?" One way that teachers use activity reinforcers is by creating a schedule in which an enjoyable activity follows the behavior they are working to modify. For example, Mr. Axton is working to reinforce cooperative behavior at cleanup time. He prompts the children, "Work together," and adds the explanation, "We'll be done faster if we all work together." Cleanup time is followed by playground time. Mr. Axton points out that "The sooner we finish, the more time we'll have to play outside." In this case, playground time is apparently an effective activity reinforcer: The children work together to complete cleanup quickly.

The following is an example of another use of an activity reinforcer.

Miranda is a 5-year-old participant in a mixed-age kindergarten-primary classroom. Miranda is very shy and hesitant to initiate toward peers. Recognizing how much Miranda enjoys being read to, her teacher designates three older girls as book buddies for Miranda. During a specified period of the day, Miranda is encouraged to approach one of her buddies and ask, "Would you please read with me?" The book buddies have agreed that if Miranda makes the request of one of them, that book buddy will read a story to Miranda in the book corner.

In this case, the desirable activity (being read to) is naturally contingent upon Miranda's practicing a social behavior that is a challenge for her.

Tangible Reinforcers. Teachers sometimes use tangible reinforcers to strengthen or modify the social behavior of children with severe problems (Vaughn, Bos, & Schumm, 1997). Tangible reinforcers include stickers, prizes, trinkets, and tokens (objects like poker chips that can be exchanged for social, activity, or other tangible rewards). Consider this example:

Myrna is a member of Ms. Andrea's preschool class. Myrna, who has experienced physical abuse and is currently in foster care, is very socially withdrawn. She rarely interacts with other children. Ms. Andrea has tried a variety of strategies to increase Myrna's rate of social interaction, including group affection activities, prompting, praise, modeling appropriate entry and response behaviors, and PALS centers. These are in addition to a comprehensive intervention plan being implemented through a transdisciplinary team collaboration, to increase Myrna's trust and self-confidence, and to help ameliorate anxiety stemming from her history of abuse.
Ms. Andrea has, however, seen only minimal change in the frequency of Myrna's peer interaction. Because she has observed the most success when Myrna participates in PALS center activities, Ms. Andrea (in consultation with her team colleagues) decides to implement a series of these activities for Myrna, during which she will be given tangible rewards for responses and initiations to peers. Aware of Myrna's love of Telletubbies [a television show], Miss Andrea awards a Telletubby sticker to Myrna each time she interacts with a peer during PALS center, stating with a smile, "You're being a friend." As a result, Myrna's rate of interaction during PALS Centers increases measurably.

One major advantage of tangible reinforcers is that they typically result in quick behavioral change, even when other strategies have failed (Alberto & Troutman, 1990). Although tangible reinforcers can be used quite effectively, their use in early childhood classrooms has been controversial. Such reinforcers can be intrusive; their effective use requires substantial teacher time and commitment. Given these disadvantages, it is important to accompany tangible reinforcers with social reinforcers. As a child exhibits the desired behavior consistently, the tangible reinforcers can be tapered off. In time, the social reinforcers can also be faded as children begin to assume control of their own behaviors (Duncan, Kemple, & Smith, 2000). Guidelines for use of reinforcement are presented in Figure 6.1.

Reinforcement and Intrinsic Motivation. Another concern that has been raised about use of reinforcement in general (and tangible reinforcers in particular) is the possibility of damaging children's intrinsic motivation

Figure 6.1. Guidelines for Using Reinforcers

1. Reinforcers are unique to an individual. There are no universal reinforcers. What one child finds reinforcing, another child may not. Therefore, teachers must consider a child's interests when selecting an appropriate reinforcer.

2. Reinforcers must be perceived by the child as being worth the time and energy it takes to achieve them. In other words, the reinforcer must be more desirable to the child than the behavior the teacher is attempting to modify.

3. Teacher expectations must be clear to the child. The child must clearly understand what specific behaviors are expected and know what is required to earn a reinforcer.

4. Reinforcers should be awarded soon after the desired behavior in order to be effective. When using reinforcement as a social skills intervention, it is important to wait until a social interaction has completely stopped before awarding reinforcement.

5. More natural reinforcers should be used whenever possible. Teachers should first consider the most normalized reinforcer to modify children's behavior. For example, social reinforcers should be used before tangible reinforcers.

6. Tangible reinforcers should be considered as a final resort, either because more natural reinforcers have been unsuccessful, or because it is necessary to eliminate a dangerous or destructive behavior immediately.

7. Reinforcers should be used less frequently and/or less predictability when the desired behavior has been established. The use of reinforcement should gradually be withdrawn.

Modified from Duncan, Kemple, and Smith. (2000).

to engage in a particular desired behavior. When children are "intrinsically motivated," they engage in a behavior or activity for its own sake. Intrinsic motivation comes from within the children or from within the behavior or activity in which they are involved (Eisenberger & Cameron, 1996). "Extrinsic motivation" refers to motivation that is outside the childen, or outside the behavior or activity in which they are involved. Externally administered rewards are frequently used to create extrinsic motivation.

Some observers and researchers have suggested that the use of reinforcers undermines intrinsic motivation (Kohn, 1993; Lepper & Greene, 1975). A well-known series of experiments was conducted in the 1970s to examine the effect of offering a child a tangible reward to engage in an initially interesting task. The results of these studies suggested that extrinsic rewards can lower intrinsic motivation (Lepper & Greene, 1975). When reinforcement is withdrawn after increasing a particular behavior (for example, withdrawal of reward stickers after increasing children's engagement in an art activity), the individual may engage in the activity less often than before the reinforcement was introduced (Eisenberger & Cameron, 1996).

However, recent research offers alternative conclusions. A meta-analysis of over 20 years of research has concluded that a tangible reward system that is contingent upon children's performance will not negatively impact children's intrinsic motivation. This comprehensive analysis suggests that the negative effects of tangible rewards occur under limited conditions, like giving tangible rewards with disregard to children's performance level (Cameron & Pierce, 1996).

When used appropriately (i.e., contingent upon children's behavior), tangible rewards may even help to increase a child's intrinsic motivation for a particular behavior. This can occur because the positive or negative experiences surrounding a behavior or activity are likely to color the child's perception of the activity as intrinsically enjoyable or unpleasant (Eisenberger & Cameron, 1996). For example, Myrna's motivation to engage with peers may be enhanced not simply because engaging with peers is a means to a desired end (the Telletubby stickers) but because pairing the sticker with interaction creates a pleasant "aura" around the interaction itself. The memory of the interaction becomes inextricably tied up with a happy feeling. An accumulation of such paired associations may ultimately increase the intrinsic appeal of peer interaction for Myrna, increase the frequency of her interactions, and thereby allow more opportunities to experience the true natural intrinsic rewards of positive peer play. With withdrawal of the telletubby stickers and continuation of the natural rewards of engagement with peers, Myrna may become "caught" in a web of natural reinforcement for peer interaction.

As noted in Figure 6.1, tangible reinforcers should be considered (1) after other forms of intervention have been deemed inadequate, (2) when immediate behavioral change is mandated because of issues of imminent physical or psychological harm, or (3) when the behavior to be developed is not currently intrinsically reinforcing to the child (Duncan, Kemple, & Smith, 2000). For example, a child who hits other children in order to obtain desired toys may find the reward of immediately getting what he wants (even if he doesn't always get to keep it for long) more intrinsically rewarding than the results of the positive social behavior of asking for a turn. The child who elicits hoots, hollers, attention, and social prestige when he calls certain peers insulting names may find those intrinsic social rewards more appealing than the suggestion that people may like him better in the long run if he refrains from such insults. The child who derives the intrinsic pleasure of sensory stimulation when she engages in "expressive aggression" by stroking and tugging a peer's silky hair may not be intrinsically motivated by the possibility of pleasing the teacher who requests that she cease, nor by the suggested substitution of stroking a doll's hair instead. In these cases, the introduction of extrinsic reinforcers for the desired prosocial behaviors is unlikely to diminish these children's intrinsic motivation to engage in those prosocial behaviors, either because they are not currently motivated toward those behaviors or because the intrinsic reward of the aggressive behavior outweighs the intrinsic reward of the prosocial behavior. For these reasons, tangible rewards may be needed to create behavioral change.

Direct Social Skills Training

A direct instructional approach to enhancing children's peer competence is the use of social skills training programs. In explicit social skills training, teachers describe and demonstrate specific social skills, and children practice or role-play the skills (Kohler & Strain, 1999; Malmskog & McDonnell, 1999; McGinnis & Goldstein, 1990; Mize, 1995; Odom, McConnell, & McEvoy, 1999). The expectation is that children will then generalize the skills learned and practiced in the instructional setting and use them in play activities in a natural setting. In general, research strongly suggests that social skills taught in instructional settings need to be paired with teacher prompts and reinforcement in natural play settings, in order to generalize to those settings (Odom & Brown, 1993). There are a number of social skills training programs that have been shown to be effective. Below, I will describe three such programs and provide sources for several others.

I Can Problem Solve. The program entitled I Can Problem Solve (ICPS): An Interpersonal Cognitive Problem-Solving Program exists in versions for preschool, kindergarten, primary, and intermediate elementary grades (Shure, 1992). The ICPS approach is based on a model that views children's social competence as best defined as a set of interrelated interpersonal problem-solving skills, which include

- Being sensitive to or recognizing interpersonal problems
- Generating alternative solutions to social problems
- Considering explicit means to achieve social goals (means-to-end thinking)
- Articulating consequences of social acts and generating alternative consequences to acts of social significance before deciding how to behave (causal thinking)
- Identifying and understanding the motives and behaviors of others

The program provides flexible scripts intended to be implemented by teachers with small groups of children (six to eight) on a daily basis. An important component of the approach is dialoguing, or the process by which teachers provide support for children to apply the skills learned in training groups to real-life problems as they occur in the classroom. The impact of ICPS training on skills and behavioral adjustment has been substantiated by 30 years of research (see, for example, Denham & Almeida, 1987). The sample teacher script that follows illustrates the introduction of an ICPS lesson in learning to generate multiple solutions to a social problem. This lesson would be introduced after the concepts of *fair*, *all*, *not*, *why*, and *because* have been taught through previous lessons. The following list shows a context in which the meanings of these words are taught to children.

(The Teacher shows a drawing depicting a little girl walking out the door and waving good-bye, while leaving another girl with a mess to clean up.)

- "Let's pretend these girls were playing with these toys (point), and it's time to put them away.
- There is a problem here. A problem is when something is wrong—something is the matter.
- Let's pretend this girl (point to the girl walking away) is going to leave and won't help this girl (point to the other girl) put the toys away.
- Now remember, both girls were playing with the toys.
- Was this girl (point to the first girl) playing?
- Was this girl (point to the second girl) playing?
- Who should help put the toys away?
- Is it *fair* for this girl (point to the girl standing by the toys) to put *all* of the toys away and for this girl (point to the girl walking away) *not* to help?
- Is it fair for both girls to help clean up?
- WHY is it FAIR for both girls to help clean up? *because* _____.
- Yes, it is *fair* for both girls to help clean up *because* they were both playing.
- So the problem is that this girl (point to the girl walking away) will *not* help clean up, put the toys away.
- Now, what can this girl (point to the girl standing by toys) do or say so the other girl will help her put the toys away?
- I'm going to write ALL your ideas on the chalkboard. Let's fill up the whole board."

(Shure, 1992, pp. 157–158)

Skillstreaming. Another explicit social skills training program is Skillstreaming, which was developed for use in early childhood (McGinnis & Goldstein, 1990) and elementary school (McGinnis & Goldstein, 1999). For early childhood, the authors provide guidelines for lessons to teach each of 40 prosocial competencies to young children in either large or small groups. The lessons can also be adapted for one-on-one individual training.

The basic components of the Skillstreaming approach are modeling, role playing, performance feedback, and transfer training. These are described for children in introductory sessions as "First we'll show you how to do a skill (modeling), then you will get to try it (role-playing), and we'll talk about how well you did (performance feedback). Then you'll get to practice it (transfer training)." (McGinnis & Goldstein, 1990, p. 75). Figure 6.2 depicts steps involved in the prosocial skill of asking someone to play and suggests situations for role play.

Recall Rocky from an earlier example in this chapter. As indicated in the narrative, prior to supporting Rocky's toy-request behavior through prompts and reinforcement, Mr. Ian used a direct training approach with Rocky. Recall that "Rocky's teacher, Mr. Ian, has worked individually with Rocky, utilizing explanation, demonstration, and role play to instruct him to use a child's first name followed by a request to bring a desired toy." The following illustration shows how the Skillstreaming approach could be used in this situation.

In a group of four children (Rocky and three peers with whom, or in proximity to whom, he plays), Mr. Ian introduces the skill of asking for assistance to reach materials. Ian asks the four children to think of particular situations in which they might need to use this skill. Mr. Ian then asks open-ended and probing questions to help the children consider some other situations they may not have thought of in which this skill could be used.

Figure 6.2. Asking Someone to Play

Steps

1. *Decide if you want to.* Discuss how to decide whether the child wants someone to play with or would rather play alone. Point out that there might be times when the child would rather be alone.

2. *Decide who.* Talk about whom the child might choose (e.g., someone who is playing alone, someone new in the class the child would like to get to know, or someone who isn't busy).

3. *Ask.* Discuss and practice ways to ask.

Suggested Situations

School: The child wants to ask a brother, sister, or parent to play.

Home: The child wants to ask a brother, sister, or parent home to play.

Peer group: The child wants to play with a friend in the neighborhood.

Adapted from McGinnis and Goldstein (1990).

Mr. Ian then presents the behavioral steps involved in asking for assistance to reach materials, which are as follows:

1. Think about whether you really need help. Can you find a way to do it yourself?
2. Think about who could help you. Who is close by? Will they be able to reach what you need? Will they be able to bring what you need?
3. Plan what to say. Think of several possible ways to ask for assistance. (Mr. Ian might also encourage the children to think about adding a reason to their request.) Remember to say the person's name first, so it is clear that you are talking to him or her. For example, "Tameeka, would you please reach the Legos for me? I want to play Legos with you." Or "Tameeka, can you push the Legos closer to me, please? I cannot reach them from my wheelchair."
4. After making a plan, make the request with a friendly look and a friendly voice.
5. Then say "thank you" or "thanks anyway" depending on the response you receive.

After introducing children to all of the steps involved in requesting help to reach materials, Mr. Ian models two examples. He enlists a skillful child to play the other character in the modeling scenario. He thinks aloud through those steps of the skill that would ordinarily be silent. For example, he says, "I want to play with those Legos, but I can't reach them. Tameeka is close to me and close to the Legos. I think she could reach them and bring them to me. Hmmm, what could I say to her?" After modeling this whole scenario, and then giving a second similar example, Mr. Ian guides the children through role playing similar scenarios, in the blocks and Legos area. After completion of role playing, Mr. Ian seeks feedback from all children in the group by asking questions like, "Did you get what you wanted?" and "Did you understand what he was telling you?" He provides reinforcement at the earliest appropriate opportunity, using praise that targets specific aspects of performance, "You used a friendly voice and a smile when you said that."

Play Time/Social Time. Designed to be used in settings with both abled and disabled children, Play Time/Social Time is another social skills training program (Odom & McConnell, 1993). This well-supported program can be used with children aged 3–5 as well as with older children with delays and/or who have significant social skills deficits. Play Time/ Social Time targets the following six social interaction skills:

1. *Sharing*—offering toys or materials to initiate peer play and interaction
2. *Persistence*—maintaining efforts to initiate social interaction
3. *Requests to share*—asking other children for help, to initiate play or interaction
4. *Play organizing*—suggesting specific activities or themes to other children for play or interaction
5. *Agreeing*—agreeing with others or offering positive responses to social initiations of others
6. *Helping*—giving or requesting assistance to other children

Play Time/Social Time provides very specific suggestions for activities, prompts, and reinforcement; includes a specified program for supporting generalization; and can be adapted for individuals.

Other Programs. Readers interested in learning about additional social skills training programs can pursue the following: The Cognitive Social Learning Curriculum (Mize, 1995; Mize & Ladd, 1990); The Buddy Skills Training Program (English, Goldstein, Shafer, & Kaczmarek, 1997; Goldstein, English, Shafer, & Kaczmarek, 1997); and Second Step (Committee for Children, 2002).

Peer-Mediated Interventions

In peer-mediated interventions, adults teach a peer or group of peers to provide encouragement to a particular child for a specific social behavior. The teacher's involvement, in this type of intervention, is with the selected peer or peers rather than with the target child. The teacher may closely monitor the intervention procedures, but does not intervene directly with the target child. An advantage of peer-mediated intervention is that the reinforcement to the target child emanates from the peer-environment, thus making it a more natural form of reinforcement. Because the teacher does not directly reinforce or prompt the child with a disability, there is no need for systematic fading of reinforcement in this type of intervention. The effectiveness of peer-mediated interventions has been supported in a variety of studies (Kohler & Strain, 1990, 1999; Odom, Chandler, Ostrosky, McConnell, & Reaney, 1992).

Peer-mediated interventions are typically carried out in several steps. The adult selects a socially competent child (or children) to serve as the intervener or "confederate." When choosing a peer as an intervention agent, it is important that the adult consider the popularity and competence of the child, his or her ability to follow directions, and desire to participate (Odom & Strain, 1986). The adult conducts training sessions to teach the socially competent child social behaviors that elicit or support the interactions of the target child. These sessions generally include a combination of verbal instruction, adult modeling, role playing, and rehearsal. Strategies that peers have been taught to use to initiate interaction with children with disabilities include offering or requesting assistance, organizing play (by suggesting or directing a play activity), showing affection, offering or requesting to share objects, and acting with persistence until initiation elicits a response from the peer with a disability. Peer confederates have also been taught to establish joint focus of attention by asking the target child to look at a toy, engaging in descriptive talk by describing his or her own play activities and the play of others, establishing eye contact by tapping on the arm or saying the child's name, and redirecting play activity (Goldstein & Wickstrom, 1986).

After training sessions, the trained peer is asked to play with the child or children with disabilities. The adult then provides prompts and reinforcement to the peer intervener for using intervention behaviors in the natural play setting. Adult prompting and reinforcing of the confederate child appears to be important to the success of peer-mediated intervention. Consider the following example:

Javon, age 6, walks and talks but has difficulty being understood due to his cerebral palsy. He quickly gives up if his attempts to initiate play aren't interpreted correctly or responded to by his peers. Ms. Hensley, Javon's teacher, uses role-playing situations to teach a group of his peers to respond to his verbalizations by checking what he means (for a sample script illustrating how Ms. Hensley might do this, see Figure 6.3).

Ms. Hensley targets discovery, math manipulative, and outdoor areas as activities in which the small-group peers and Javon have similar interests and motivation to interact. Also, she chooses several activities so that Javon and his peers will have more opportunities to practice, maintain, and generalize their skills. After teaching a small group of peers in role-playing sessions, she now rewards the children during naturally occurring daily play by holding up a happy face puppet immediately after peers appropriately react to Javon's attempts at communication and when he responds to turns in play situations. Then she puts a happy face sticker on each child's helper card. Periodically throughout the day, she shows the children the cards and verbally praises their appropriate behaviors. Initially, the children will earn extra computer time based on their happy face cards. She will then fade this reinforcement of the peer confederates.

Figure 6.3. Sample Script: Training Peer Confederates

TEACHER: Have you noticed that sometimes it is hard to understand what Javon is saying to you?

BRETT AND TITO: Yes.

TEACHER: Can you remember some times that happened? Can you tell me about it?

BRETT: Well, like today he wouldn't say the right words.

TEACHER: Yes, sometimes it is hard for Javon to say the words he wants to say. Do you remember what he said?

BRETT: (Shrugs) Just some noises, and about a car.

TEACHER: About a car? Were you guys playing with cars?

BRETT: Yeah, we were at the rug, and he said "cah."

TEACHER: I am going to teach you some things you can say to Javon, when you don't understand him. When you say these things, it might help him to tell you what he means. (Teacher goes and gets a box of cars.)

TEACHER: Let's pretend you guys are each playing with a car, and there is this box of cars on the shelf. I'll pretend I am Javon.

TEACHER (as Javon): Ah pay cah. Pay cah.

TITO: You said cah. (laughs) You said "car."

TEACHER: You think I said "car." If you think Javon said car (remember I am pretending I'm Javon), you could just say to him "car"? Did you say "car," Javon?

TITO: Well, OK.

TEACHER: Say it. Pretend I am Javon and say it to me. First I say "Ah pay 'cah.'"

TITO: You said "car," Javon?

TEACHER (as Javon): (Nods head, smiles slightly, and reaches). Cah. Ah pay.

BRETT: Hey, she wants the car.

TEACHER: What could you say to me? I'm Javon. What could you say?

TITO: You want the car?

TEACHER (as Javon): (Nods head yes.)

TITO: (Hands her the car.)

TEACHER: Guys, that was great! You heard "cah" and you thought maybe I said "car." So you said, "You said 'car' Javon?" Then you noticed that maybe I wanted to play with it. You said, "You want the car?" That is very good. You helped me tell you what I wanted to say!
(Tito and Brett nod)

TEACHER: When you thought you understood that "cah" meant "car," you said the word right out loud to me. You said "car." That's great. That helped me. That helped me know that you understood.

Figure 6.3. (*continued*)

TEACHER: Let's try one more. I'm being Javon again. (Teacher holds car and scoots it back and forth) "Leh may groad."

TITO AND BRETT: (look at each other and shrug and grimace, then are silent)

TEACHER: When I am Javon, now, I am thinking, "Those guys don't want to play with me."

BRETT: We don't know what you said.

TITO: Those aren't real words.

TEACHER (as Javon): (looking around) Leh may groad.

TITO AND BRETT: (laughter)

TEACHER: Can you understand any of my words?

TITO AND BRETT: *No*!

TEACHER: If you can't understand any of Javon's words, here is a thing you can do. (Leans in close to emphasize the importance of what she is about to say.) You can say one of the sounds that you heard me say. One of the words, say it just like it sounded. Try it. I said "Leh may groad."

BRETT: Okay . . . groad.

TEACHER: Good! You can say to me, "Javon, you said groad?" Say it.

BRETT: Javon, you said "groad?"

TEACHER (as Javon): (laughs) Road! Leh may groad!

BRETT: Hey, I think you said "let's make a road!"

TEACHER (as Javon): Yah!!! Leh mayg eh road!

TEACHER: Alright! Now I feel really good! You guys understood! What happened here?

BRETT: I understood him.

TEACHER: Yes. I said "leh may groad." First you didn't understand. Then what did you do? . . . You said a word I made that you didn't understand. You said . . . what?

BRETT: Groad.

TEACHER: And when I was being Javon, I thought "That was funny. He said 'groad' instead of road!" So I said "Road. Leh mayg eh road."

TITO AND BRETT: Ha!

TEACHER: So, you helped me say what I wanted to say. You guys are doing a great job! Before, when I said "cah," you thought maybe I said "car" so you said "did you say car," right?

TITO: Right.

(*continued*)

Figure 6.3. (*continued*)

TEACHER: Then, when you didn't know what I said, you said one of the words I tried to say, just like it sounded. You said "Groad."
   That helped me say what I was trying to say.
   So these are two things you can do if you don't understand. (Holds up one finger for emphasis) You can say a word that you *think* you understand. Or (holds up second finger) if you can't understand anything, you can say a word that you heard, just exactly the way you heard it.

BRETT AND TITO: OK.

TEACHER: You can do that with Javon. That would be a way to help him. Sometimes it might work, but sometimes it might not. You'll have to try it lots of times. Even if it doesn't work one time, you try it again the next time. Whenever I see you try it, I'll put a happy face sticker on your helper card. I'll hold up a happy face puppet just to let you know I'm gonna put a sticker on your card. Do you guys think you can do this, to help Javon?

BRETT: Yep.

TITO: Sure.

Peer-mediated interventions, which have been used successfully with children as young as preschool age, require considerable skill on the part of the adult. Peer-mediated intervention will be further discussed in Chapter 7 with regard to children with autism spectrum disorders.

MAXIMIZING SUCCESS

To maximize the success of the higher-intensity interventions described in this chapter, several principles and strategies should be considered. First, always consider these within the framework of a hierarchy of least to most natural and intensive approaches. In a majority of cases, higher-intensity interventions will likely be unnecessary; instead, environmental changes or naturalistic interventions may be effective. Also, remember that the higher tier of the hierarchy is supported by the foundation of the lower tiers. Direct and explicit instruction in social skills, for example, is unlikely to increase children's peer competence if that instruction isn't couched within an environment and a web of naturalistic teaching strategies that are designed to support peer interaction.

   A commonly noted weakness of approaches that are centered in direct instruction of social skills is that, while such interventions often show great success in altering children's social behavior in the training setting, newly acquired social skills often do not generalize to and continue in the natural setting (Chandler, Lubeck, & Fowler, 1992). Three basic types of strategies can be useful to support generalization and maintenance of newly learned social behaviors. These have been termed as (1) taking advantage of natural communities of reinforcement, (2) training diversely, and (3) incorporating functional mediators (Brown & Odom, 1994). Brief descriptions and examples of these are provided below (for further information and detail, see Brown & Odom, 1994).

Taking advantage of natural communities of reinforcement simply means capitalizing upon the reinforcing value of typical social consequences in the classroom. For example, when Omar shares a toy with a peer, his sharing behavior may be naturally reinforced by a pleasant reciprocal interaction with that peer. After his teacher has used prompting and praising to teach Omar sharing behavior, and has thereby introduced him to the natural web of classroom contingencies, those natural consequences themselves can come to reinforce Omar's behavior as the teacher systematically withdraws her prompts and praise. Group affection activities, which were described in Chapter 5, may help to support generalization of newly trained skills. In a sense, group affection activities serve as an "icebreaker," putting children into contact with peers through the playful practice of social skills that have a high likelihood of eliciting positive social responses.

Training diversely means providing social skills training in a diverse range of circumstances and conditions. The generalization of behaviors to the natural setting can be enhanced by using more than one trainer (for example, the classroom teacher, the classroom assistant, and the special education liaison teacher) and/or involving several different peers in training sessions. "Training loosely" within the relatively uncontrolled setting of the natural classroom (as opposed to relying on training in a separate room with only one or two peers) can aid in generalization and maintenance of behavior because the training itself incorporates many of the stimuli of the natural environment. For example, teaching Matilda initiation skills in a small room down the hall, with John and Harriet as participating peers, may result in Matilda's ability to use those skills with John and Harriet in the little room. When she returns to the classroom, however, the social and physical setting is so dissimilar to the setting in which she learned the skills that Matilda is unable to use those skills reliably even with adult prompting and reinforcement. Continuing the training during free play time within the classroom (or even conducting initial training during free play time) and incorporating many peers in Matilda's sessions avoids the likelihood of Matilda's behavior being partially under control of the unique stimuli of the artificial training setting of the little room.

Another way of training diversely is to make the connection between the child's behavior and the reinforcer less apparent to the child. For example, Matilda's initiation behaviors can be helped to occur (and to continue to occur) in the natural environment if her teacher stops reinforcing Matilda for every instance of the targeted behavior, or delays the reinforcement. The teacher can also gradually fade her prompts for Matilda's behavior, and take care to reinforce Matilda for spontaneous initiations that are *not* prompted by the teacher.

Incorporating functional mediators means intentionally incorporating common environmental stimuli or verbal behavior in training sessions that can facilitate generalization of children's newly learned behaviors to natural settings and circumstances (Brown & Odom, 1994). For example, Matilda's teacher may teach her the self-management technique of "verbal correspondence." That is, she teaches Matilda to tell her, at the beginning of a play session, what she is going to do to initiate play, like "I am going to say 'let's play witches' to Sally." After the play session, the teacher may remind Matilda of her plan, and ask her to report back to her what she did say to Sally. Matilda's teacher reinforces her for accurate reports of the behavior. In this way, by linking words with action plans, Matilda becomes more aware of her behavior and of her ability to act planfully.

Another way of using functional mediators is to intentionally provide commonalities between a training setting and the setting in which the behavior is to be applied. In one study, it was demonstrated that the imitative behavior of children with autism is generalized across settings and that this generalization is related to the presence of particular furniture or gestures made by the trainers during the training sessions (Rincouer & Koegel, 1975, as cited in Brown & Odom, 1994).

Higher-intensity interventions have been supported by research as effective in teaching new behaviors, and techniques exist that can help newly acquired skills generalize and be maintained within the natural classroom setting. However, it is important to note that the success of these interventions has been demonstrated in research studies in which the trainer(s) were researchers or teachers highly trained by the research team. This highlights the importance of professional collaboration described in Chapter 2. Higher-intensity interventions typically require the expertise and support of an interdisciplinary team of professionals working together.

SUMMARY

Direct training in social skills, peer-mediated strategies to encourage responsiveness and engagement, as well as prompting/reinforcement as components to maximize the success of these approaches, are important tools for teachers to know. For some children with significant social difficulties (including children with and without disabilities), these more intensive interventions may be warranted. As will be described in Chapter 7, children with significant social difficulties can also benefit from modes of intervention and support at the less intensive levels of the hierarchy. Sometimes these less intensive interventions may be sufficient. At other times less intensive interventions may provide necessary foundation and support for the use of more directed, intensive interventions.

FOOD FOR THOUGHT

1. Review the story of Javier at the opening of this chapter. Let's assume that Javier's aggressive behavior has significantly diminished as an apparent result of the token reinforcement system. Let's also assume that careful observation has revealed that Javier is interested in peer interaction and establishing friendships, does not seem to be shy or lacking in self-confidence, but lacks skill in ways of letting peers know that he would like to play with them.

   - How might Mrs. Bowen "wean" Javier from the token reinforcement system?
   - How might Mrs. Bowen implement an intervention to help Javier learn to initiate play activities with peers?
   - What other methods of support and intervention might Mrs. Bowen use, and why?

2. Both independence as an individual and ability to function as a member of the group are part of every culture, though in some cultures one has higher priority than the other. In group-oriented cultures, the use of individual praise may be seen as placing undue emphasis on the individual, on his or her uniqueness, and on personal pride.

   - As a teacher, how might your use of reinforcement be guided by your knowledge of the various cultural backgrounds of the children in your class?
   - Reconsider the plan of action developed for Javier by Mrs. Bowen and Ms. Janowitz. If the adults know that Javier's cultural background downplays focus on the individual, how might they decide to modify this plan to be a better cultural match for Javier?

CHAPTER 7

Supporting Children with Particular Social Needs and Disabilities

Decisions about support and intervention are best made on the basis of an individual child's social competence needs. No prescription exists for addressing the needs of "the shy child," "the aggressive child," or "the child with visual impairment." Intervention decisions cannot be made on a categorical basis because every child is unique, every child's strengths are unique, and every child's needs are unique. There is no substitute for knowing the individual child through interaction and observation within the social arena of the classroom. For children with significant needs, this observation and decision making will often involve the collaboration of a team of professionals. Within a framework of individualized attention, it is helpful to recognize that specific social needs and challenges are often (though not always) associated with particular child characteristics and particular disabling conditions. In this chapter, some of these needs will be identified along with promising methods of support and intervention for children with particular needs.

It is useful to recognize that children with particular needs may also possess complementary or compensatory strengths. A shy child may be a keen observer, a child with a visual impairment may have heightened capacity to gain social information through hearing, and a child who is deaf may be highly sensitive to nuances in facial expression and posture. It is, however, imperative to attune to idiosyncratic strengths of individual children and to incorporate those in plans for intervention, rather than making stereotypical guesses about individual strengths based on individual disabilities or needs.

CHILDREN WHO OFTEN FEEL SHY

Virtually everyone feels shy from time to time. Shyness is often provoked in novel situations and situations with a perceived evaluative component. Individuals vary with regard to their tendency to respond in a shy manner. These individual differences can be attributed to a combination of genetic predispositions and experiential factors. Shyness is often evident in very early childhood and can impact children's peer relationships and interaction skills by keeping the child on the sidelines of the social arena in which social skills and relationships are practiced and developed (Swallow, 2000).

In social situations, shy young children often feel anxious, resistant, and fearful of making a mistake, of being unfavorably evaluated, and of looking foolish. Shy children are often torn between conflicting motivations: the desire for social involvement and friendship versus the fear of social interaction. In the preschool years, this motivational conflict often manifests itself through "hovering" behavior. A child who is shy can often be seen floating on the outskirts of social activity, watching with quiet anxiety. This wait-and-watch approach can be a good strategy prior to entering into a social group, but shy children tend to hover too long, increasing their own anxiety and decreasing their likelihood of eventually being integrated into the activity (Rubin & Asendorf, 1993). In the primary grades as children become more reflective and cognitively mature, their anxiety and self-consciousness often heighten. Social status becomes an issue in the primary grades as children become consciously aware of who is popular and who is not.

In the early childhood years, a frequently shy child may or may not lack social skills. When a teacher considers how to help a shy child fit into the social world of the classroom, it is important to consider the difference between competence and performance. A shy child may possess a good deal of knowledge about the social world and interaction "know-how" but feel too fearful or self-conscious to put into practice what he or she knows.

This distinction is important because teaching skills to a child who already possesses them may not be a good use of time, whereas providing confidence-enhancing experiences may enable the child to begin to use and practice his or her possessed skills. To determine whether a child's difficulty is more a problem of confidence or competence, it can be helpful to observe the child in situations in which he or she generally feels very comfortable (perhaps with a very familiar peer or in a small group in a familiar setting). In these "safe" settings a shy child may reveal a surprising level of competence and awareness. Ultimately, if a child does not gain the confidence to become involved and use and practice interaction skills, he or she is likely to fall behind in peer social skills and social knowledge because these capacities are strengthened and refined within the peer social world itself (Rubin & Asendorf, 1993).

To bolster a shy child's confidence and comfort level, teachers can structure opportunities for the child to interact in small groups with supportive peers. Because shy children are often uncomfortable in very open-ended situations in which they do not know what behavior is expected of them, provision of PALS-type centers and cooperative learning experiences can provide a comforting level of structure to an anxious and self-conscious child. Sometimes opportunities to play with a gentle younger child can give a shy child a chance to be the "big guy," to show the ropes and feel a sense of his or her own capabilities. Similarly, opportunities to be the expert can boost a shy child's confidence. A child who has a special strength or interest can be invited to share that with other children. This may even be essentially nonverbal sharing: tying shoes for peers who are not yet able, showing a special collection from home and responding to a few simple questions that can be answered with a nod or shake of the head, demonstrating a skill like turning cartwheels. Teachers can suggest that parents help their child learn to engage in affirming self-talk. Shy children can be taught to replace their frequently negative self-talk ("All the kids will laugh at me." "I'm stupid.") with positive self-messages ("I can do this." "I'm a great kid." "People like to play with me."). (For suggestions about teaching positive self-talk, see Swallow, 2000.)

Group affection activities as identified in Chapter 5 can be a very useful strategy for a child who is socially withdrawn. These activities serve as an icebreaker, providing peer contact through the medium of a structured, nonthreatening, and playful activity. Group affection activities also serve as opportunities to practice important social behaviors. They are particularly conducive to practicing skills of making contact and showing interest and affection, and are therefore well suited to common needs of shy children.

Peer mediated approaches, as described in Chapter 6, have also been demonstrated to work well for many socially withdrawn children (Odom et al., 1992). These can be used to teach a peer-confederate child to use initiation strategies like taking the shy child's hand and asking the child to play, suggesting specific play ideas, offering to share toys, asking the peer to share toys, and offering help. These strategies provide the shy child with a chance to become engaged without the "risk" of making the initiation, and also serve as a model of good initiation strategies. Shy children who lack social skills may also benefit from opportunities to interact in structured pairing or trios, including a highly socially competent and patient peer who may serve as a model of skillful behavior.

Children who are frequently shy are typically introverted and therefore easily overwhelmed by unrelenting social stimulation. It is particularly important to provide "down time" and places for quiet individual retreat to enable such children to refuel their engines, as described in Chapter 3. Many psychologists and educators have stressed the importance of avoiding the "shy" label; labeling a child in any way can cause self-consciousness, impact self-perceptions, and ultimately become a self-perpetuating prophecy. It may be more helpful instead to talk with all children about "feeling shy." Shyness is a human response. Everyone feels shy from time to time, and therefore everyone can have some understanding of shyness as a personality style. Finally, teachers can help children who experience frequent shyness by providing resources to their parents. Parents are often concerned about their shy child's behavior, and resources such as Honig (1987) and Swallow (2000) can provide welcome support and suggestions for parenting such children.

CHILDREN WITH AGGRESSIVE BEHAVIOR PATTERNS

Young children may behave in aggressive ways for a multitude of reasons. "Expressive aggression" is a term used to describe those incidences of aggression in which children engage for the purpose of seeking sensory stimulation or release: the child's intention is not to cause harm, though harm may result. Expressive aggression has occurred when Casey tugs sharply on Melody's long, silky hair because she like the way it feels between her fingers; when Hugo simultaneously hugs, pummels, and knocks down his friend Clarence in a whirlwind of unbridled exuberance; when Tessa repeatedly bump, bump, bumps then shoves Brian in line because she is bored, restless, tired of waiting, and needs to move.

"Instrumental aggression" is common in the preschool years. In incidences of instrumental aggression, the child's primary purpose again is not to cause harm, but simply to get what he or she wants: a toy, a turn, attention. When Georgia pushes Petra out of the wagon and clambers in herself, Petra may be hurt as a result. If Georgia's primary intention was to have a turn in the wagon (and Petra's injury was a by-product of Georgia's actions toward her primary goal) then instrumental aggression has occurred. Young children may engage in expressive and instrumental aggression because their verbal abilities are limited, because they are limited in their knowledge or skill regarding alternative ways to get their needs met, because they are limited in their ability to recognize another child's point of view, and/or because the aggressive acts have been reinforced as they have proven effective in gaining what is wanted.

"Hostile aggression" becomes more predominant in the primary grades. Hostile aggression is carried out for the primary intention of causing physical or emotional hurt. When Austin is teased and taunted by Donnie, he lashes out in fury and kicks Donnie in the belly. Both boys' aggression may have been "hostile." Donnie's verbal aggression was intended to humiliate Austin, and Austin's physical retaliation was intended to injure Donnie in return. Understanding, preventing, and responding to aggressive behavior is a challenge and a critical responsibility of early childhood educators.

When an individual child exhibits severe or persistent aggression at school, educators have a responsibility to help that child learn more acceptable behavior and at the same time have a responsibility to protect the other children in the class. When teachers allow aggressive behavior to continue, children are left to protect themselves. They often see counterattack as their only defense. Unchecked aggression begets aggression. When aggression is ignored or allowed to continue, children feel frustrated and frightened. Teachers have a responsibility to provide a psychologically safe classroom environment. They also have an important role to play in helping the aggressive child change his or her behavior. Children with high levels of aggressive behavior are at risk of peer rejection. Early aggressive behavior is a strong predictor of later antisocial behavior, violence, and serious adjustment problems (American Psychological Association, 1993; Pepler & Slaby, 1994; Yoshikawa, 1994).

A recent review of intervention research on managing aggressive behavior in early childhood highlights the evidence that childhood aggression is difficult to treat. Virtually all intervention programs that have been successful for early childhood aggression have been those that contain traditional behavior management practices (Bryant, Vizzard, Willoughby, & Kupersmidt, 1999). Behavioral theory holds that behaviors acquired and displayed by young children can be attributed largely to their antecedents and consequences. Yet misunderstandings exist concerning the appropriate use and potential effectiveness of these strategies for young children, and they are not always well accepted in the early childhood community (Henderick, 1998; Rodd, 1996). A review of contemporary literature suggests that behavioral strategies are appropriate for creating and maintaining an environment conducive to growth and development (e.g., Schloss & Smith, 1998). Research has demonstrated that behavioral strategies are successful in school settings with various diverse populations, including those with young children (Kazdin, 1994).

A full discussion of methods of preventing and responding to aggressive behavior is beyond the scope of this book. Two excellent resources on this topic are *Early Violence Prevention: Tools for Teachers of Young Children* (Slaby et al., 1995), and *Understanding and Affecting the Behavior of Young Children* (Zirpoli, 1995). Generally speaking, the practices I described in Chapters 3, 4, and 5 help to establish a classroom ecology that encourages and acknowledges prosocial behaviors as alternative to aggression. Teachers can help to prevent aggressive behavior when they minimize the likelihood of children being rewarded for aggressive behavior, when they help to diffuse conflicts before they escalate, when they reason with children in individually developmentally appropriate ways, and when they prevent undue frustration in children's lives at school. Teachers help to reduce aggression when they implement meaningful consequences for aggression. Meaningful consequences include natural consequences, which can be pointed out to children ("You screamed at Nelson. Now he doesn't want to work with you"). They also include "logical consequences," another type of meaningful consequences, which entail making reparations ("Nicholas's knee is bleeding. Please get a bandage"; "Help Terrell gather the blocks back together so she can rebuild her city."), or which entail the immediate practice of alternate behaviors ("Tell Marco what you want. Tell him with words.") or actions that are logically related to the aggressive behavior ("You threw the sand at Cherie; Now you will have to leave the sandbox and find another place to play.").

Individualized Planning

All of these practices can be effectively used as part of a total plan for children who exhibit high levels of aggression. They are not likely to be sufficient, however. Children who engage in severe and/or persistent aggressive behavior are likely to need additional support. Effective programs for changing aggressive behavior are based on observation of the child and are tailored to that individual child's needs. A-B-C analysis (Antecedent-Behavior-Consequence) is a useful tool for observing and making sense of a child's aggressive behavior (Neilson, Olive, Donovan, & McEvoy, 1999). Figure 7.1 provides an example of a record of an A-B-C observation involving three girls during circle time.

Multiple A-B-C observations of circle time disruptions involving these

Figure 7.1. Example of an A-B-C Observation

> *Antecedent:* At the signal to start circle time, Talia ran quickly and wedged herself between Renee and Jane.
>
> *Behavior:* Renee pinched Talia on the thigh at the beginning of circle time.
>
> *Consequence:* Talia shoved Renee hard. Teacher told Talia to move to another part of the circle. Renee and Jane sidled up very close to one another and smirked across the circle at Talia.

three girls may help the teacher to see a pattern that reveals the purposes of the pinching and shoving behavior. This can provide the teacher with clues about how to most effectively intervene.

A-B-C analysis helps to reveal the circumstances that elicit aggressive behavior, as well as the consequences that serve to reward and perpetuate the aggressive behavior. A-B-C analysis may reveal, for example, whether Lenny's frequent aggressive attacks in the lunch line are a way to gain attention, relieve frustration, escape or preempt teasing by peers, or avoid standing in line. If Lenny's aggressive behavior serves the dual purposes of relieving the frustration of a long wait and escaping from that wait, then sending Lenny to "time out" by removing him from the situation would not likely be an effective intervention. Time out would actually help fulfill his purposes and reinforce the aggressive behavior.

Tangible Rewards

The use of short-term tangible reward systems can provide an effective jump start to behavioral change (Slaby et al., 1995). In Chapter 6, a tangible reward system was employed as a means of helping Javier get over the initial "hump" toward altering his aggressive behaviors, and as a way to quickly restore psychological safety to the classroom setting. Tangible reward systems can be particularly useful if a child is indifferent to teacher attention, encouragement, and other forms of social reinforcement. A young child whose aggressive behaviors far outnumber their prosocial behaviors may not yet have experienced the natural rewards of cooperative interaction. Tangible rewards can help the child get "plugged in" to positive interaction, and experience the natural rewards that ultimately can take the place of the tangible rewards. (For further discussion of tangible rewards, see Duncan et al., 2000; Slaby et al., 1995).

Time Out

Time out is a controversial practice in early childhood classrooms. Many have expressed concern about its overuse and misuse. For a child who exhibits high levels of aggression, time out can be effectively used as one form of consequence. Kostelnik et al. (2002) suggest limiting use of time out to cases of habituated aggressive behavior. Habituated aggressive behavior is aggression that persists because it is being rewarded (by attention, prestige, instrumental success, and so forth). In such cases, time out serves as "time out from reinforcement." Time out interrupts the cycle of reinforcement by removing the child from the source of reward. A short time out at the moment of aggressive behavior has been shown to be effective as part of a program to help a child learn to control aggression (Patterson & White, 1970).

Slaby et al. (1995) describe the appropriate use of time out for young children as consisting of removal to the sidelines of activity or removal to an area of the classroom away from the other children (but *never* isolation in a closed room). Upon first use for a particular behavior for a particular child, time out should be preceded by a warning to the individual child. Time out should be only a couple of moments in length, extended if the child continues to be disruptive during time out. It is suggested that the teacher wait until after the time out to talk with the child about his or her behavior, because adult attention during time out has high potential to undermine its purpose. By following these guidelines, time out can be used in a caring and supportive way as part of a behavioral change program (Slaby et al., 1995). Time out can help children control their aggressive behavior and thereby prevent peer rejection and development of a negative reputation among peers.

CHILDREN WITH VISUAL IMPAIRMENT

Challenges

Think about the challenge of integrating a young child with severe visual impairment into the social world of the classroom. Upon initial consideration, it may seem that the only concerns would revolve around appropriate structuring of the physical environment, familiarizing the child with where things are, and educating the other children about the child's special needs with regard to locating objects and areas in the classroom.

Think again, and keep in mind that an estimated 85% of the information people receive is transmitted through the visual sense. Consider the volume of social information we receive (and send out) visually through facial expressions, gestures, eye contact, and body posture. Visually transmitted information helps us to know when another has finished speaking, signaling our turn in conversation. Visual information helps us discern a speaker's humorous intent, anger, or frustration. It helps us recognize a listener's confusion or misunderstanding. Visual information helps us know when an interaction is drawing to a close. It helps us understand what a group of children are "playing about." Children with visual impairment have limited or no access to a very important source of social information. This situation significantly impacts the child's facility to learn social skills incidentally, because so much of incidental learning of social skills occurs via visual observation.

Information gained through sight helps children develop understanding of directionality, cause and effect, and intentionality. Very little information about these early concepts is transmitted through sound. In part as a result of this, young children with visual impairment tend to be more egocentric than their sighted peers. Passivity is often evident as a result: Children with visual impairment initiate interactions at far lower rates than their peers (Rogers & Puchalski, 1984).

Children who are completely blind often do not begin to walk until age 3 or 4, and typically do not crawl first. Their experience exploring their environment may be very limited. Consider how much of a sighted child's play grows out of environmental exploration. Children with severe visual impairment often have immature play skills. Because play provides an extremely important context for young children's social interactions, limited play skills can further restrict access to the world of peers for a child with visual impairment (Skellenger, Hill, & Hill, 1992).

Children with severe visual impairment who are merely physically included in an early childhood classroom may have limited access to peers at school because they tend to be inactive and passive and they have limited ability to locate their peers and sites of interaction. If they do locate these, they have difficulty moving to where the social "action" is occurring. If they do manage to move there, the location of the action may have changed by the time they get there. A young peer is a moving target! The child with severely impaired vision also may have difficulty getting peers to come to where they are, because it is hard for them to locate a peer to signal, and they have difficulty signaling their interest in interaction.

When planning support for any child, it is as important to consider the child's strengths and interests as his or her needs or disabilities. The following scenario, observed in a kindergarten class, nicely illustrates the sometimes surprising capacities of a young child with a disability.

The children in Mrs. Bronson's class had recently completed their first "published" books. Each child had created, over a period of weeks, a book about his or her family complete with illustrations and typed text. Parents were invited to a "literary tea," during which each child had the opportunity to read his or her book (into a real microphone) for the assembled audience. About halfway through came Sonny's turn. Sonny, blind since birth, turned slightly sideways toward the microphone as he read his book, which was typed in Braille. Following his text was a series of texture pictures Sonny had created, using felt, yarn, and glue. His hands skipped nimbly across each picture as he "read" the picture verbally to his audience. He turned the page to one very large and prominent picture, and announced into the microphone, "This is a big smiley face." He then turned to squarely face the audience and said with genuine amusement, "But I guess I don't need to tell *you* that!" As parental laughter rippled through the room, Sonny turned once again, with a giggle and a shrug, toward the audience and exclaimed with animation, "Yeah, I know, I crack me up too!"

The humor that Sonny employed in this situation required a rather sophisticated perspective for a 5-year-old. It is particularly noteworthy given that children who are blind often have difficulty overcoming egocentrism. This capacity to understand another person's perspective and to make people laugh is a great social strength that can be capitalized upon to support this child's continuing inclusion in the social world of his school, and to maintain his peers' acceptance.

Support and Intervention

Because a child with visual impairment often has difficulty gaining proximity to desirable peers for the purpose of social play, the creation of size-restricted play spaces can help to overcome this impediment to social interaction (Skellenger et al., 1992). The information on PALS centers, described in Chapter 5, can be used to structure contained play situations. With forethought, these opportunities can be designed to include materials that highlight the child's abilities, rather than disabilities. Teachers may initially need to be closely involved in PALS centers designed for children with severe visual impairment.

Since children with severe visual impairment cannot rely on visual cues to gain peers' attention, it is particularly important that they know the names of all their peers and be able to identify them by the sounds of their voices. Name games and circle time songs that are used to familiarize children with one another (e.g., "Who stole the cookie from the cookie jar,"

"Willoughby Wallaby Woo," "The More We Get Together") can be modified so that children speak their own names. Verbal sharing opportunities (at snack time, circle time) in which children are asked to identify themselves by name, can support name/voice recognition.

Peer-mediated approaches as described in Chapter 6 may be useful for children with visual impairment. Selected peer mediators, however, would need to have a good understanding of the ramifications of restricted visual input. It is therefore likely that an adult trainer will need to engage in extensive tutoring of the peer mediator, and the peer mediator should be a child with fairly sophisticated social-cognitive understanding. For preschool and kindergarten settings, it may be necessary to engage an older child as a peer mediator. In order to help the peer mediator learn strategies for giving the target child needed social information, an adult would need to help the peer mediator understand the absence of eye contact and of nonverbal cues, the need to initiate and respond in the *absence* of these, and how to recognize and repair breakdowns in communication (Skellenger et al., 1992).

Because children with severe visual impairment do not learn social skills through visual observational learning, direct instruction in social skills as described in Chapter 6 is likely to be necessary. Scripts for indicating interest in joining play, and instruction in social skills for attention getting, clearly directing initiations, and turn-taking can be taught through adult-led coaching and training interventions.

CHILDREN WITH HEARING IMPAIRMENT

Challenges

Children who are deaf or hard of hearing are at risk for social competence problems and difficulty in peer skills and relationships. This can occur for reasons both obvious and more subtle. Children who experience early and prolonged auditory deprivation may experience changes in the organization of the brain, impacting their cognition, behavior, and social competence (Kusche & Greenberg, 1989). This underscores the importance of early intervention for children with hearing impairment.

Children with hearing impairment have limited ability to express and understand spoken language, which makes early interaction with caregivers difficult. Severe hearing loss is often undiagnosed until a child is between 2 and 4 years of age, so children may live their very early years (years that are highly sensitive for the development of language and communication) without appropriate supports like amplification and parental use of signing. Thus, opportunities for developing social competence through parent-child interaction may be severely restricted. Furthermore, children with hearing impairment typically have limited experience in interaction with peers (Antia & Kreimeyer, 1992). These children's relative social isolation from peers and caregivers reduces their opportunities to interact and to develop social competence. This potentially creates a vicious circle, as children's limited social competence further diminishes their opportunities for interaction.

The way that adults interact with a child with hearing impairment can impede the development of social competence. Evidence suggests that parents of children with hearing impairment are more likely to employ a parental discipline style that relies on time out and physical punishment (Greenberg & Kusche, 1993). Perhaps as a result of their frustration with the challenge of communicating with the child, parents are less likely to use the inductive style of discipline that gives children opportunities to learn what they did wrong and why, how their behavior affects others, and what alternative they could have chosen. Thus, children with hearing impairment may experience fewer opportunities to develop the social cognitive abilities that contribute to prosocial dispositions and general social competence (Greenberg & Kusche, 1993).

Children with hearing impairment often receive less rich and descriptive communication from adults. Hearing adults may feel uncomfortable or less than competent as they communicate with a child through American Sign Language; after all, it is a second language for them. This reduced richness and complexity in communication for the hearing impaired child restricts the child's ability to develop a broad vocabulary and rich complex signed language (Greenberg & Kusche, 1993).

Children with hearing impairment often experience delayed language and communication development, greater impulsiveness and poorer emotion regulation, and have an impoverished vocabulary of emotion language. As a result they often have limited communication skills and diminished interpersonal problem-solving abilities (Greenberg & Kusche, 1993). Such conversational skills as turn-taking, topic maintenance, and initiation are difficult for children with hearing impairment to learn, in part because adults have a strong tendency to take over for these children and run the conversation. Furthermore, the more adults interact with the hearing impaired child in the peer environment, the less time the child spends in interaction with peers (Antia, 1982).

The degree and age of onset of hearing loss differentially affect children's communication and social challenges. Generally speaking, children with mild to moderate hearing impairment acquire spoken language more easily. Children with severe hearing loss generally learn to sign, though as mentioned this may not be taught until the diagnosis is made, as late as 4 years of age. In general, if a child's hearing loss is present at birth or occurs before the child begins to use spoken language, the child will have more difficulty developing language and communicative competence (Antia, 1994).

Intervention and Support

If a child's hearing loss is minimal, it is likely that only slight modifications to classroom practices will be needed (see Figure 7.2). Children with more severe impairment may require more intensive coaching interventions, in addition to environmental and naturalistic interventions. A child who uses signed English, American Sign Language, or who relies on cued speech (a system of hand signals to enhance lip reading) will likely need the support of a transliterator or interpreter.

Figure 7.2. Simple Social Supports for Children with Hearing Impairment

1. Teach simple functional signs to whole class

2. Give everyone a sign name, and use them

3. Provide access to the music of the classroom community: Song cards, song picture books, signed songs (or sign only the chorus), visual props, turn up the bass on recorded music

4. Use visual signals (e.g., flash the lights) and signing to support transitions and daily routines

5. Teach children to face the child with hearing impairment and not to obstruct view of their own mouth

6. Encourage all community members to speak at normal speed and volume without exaggerated lip movements

7. Establish a hand-raising habit in large and small group times to signal turn taking and facilitate communication

8. Teach all children ways of gaining peers' attention: touch on arm, speak and sign peer's name, wave, face-to-face gaze, and eye contact

9. Provide access to stories and other books (these are important parts of shared classroom culture): Team reading (e.g., one adult reads and the other signs), use signing only for repeated phrases or words, use oral/signed storytelling, flannel board

10. Designate a time each day when only signing is used

Sources: Russel-Fox (1997); Luetke-Stahlman (1994).

In light of evidence that adults tend to take over interaction with children who have a hearing impairment, teachers may want to examine and consider reducing or restructuring their role in interacting with a child with a hearing impairment. Instead of playing the role of an interaction partner, adults can resolve to more often play the role of a scaffolder or supporter to children's *peer* interaction. Teachers may also consider whether they need to modify the way they talk to a child with a hearing impairment. Encouraging the child to initiate and maintain conversation may be accomplished by adults reducing their requests for repetition, reducing their questioning, increasing their use of contributions to conversation, and providing the child time to start and finish speaking (Antia & Kreimeyer, 1992).

Intensive contact with familiar peers can play a significant role in supporting interaction between hearing children and children with hearing impairment. An effective strategy is providing 20-minute play sessions three times per week for small stable groups of both hearing and hearing impaired peers (i.e., the same children every time) without any direct adult involvement (Antia, Kreimeyer, & Eldredge, 1993). Creation of structured play opportunities like PALS centers (as described in Chapter 5) with a teacher available to model, interpret, and use various incidental teaching strategies may also be a promising way to develop social skills in children with hearing impairment and increase interaction with hearing peers.

Peer-mediated interventions as described in Chapter 6 have been used successfully to teach confederates many skills that seem to be important for engaging children with hearing impairment. These include establishing eye contact, establishing joint focus of attention, redirecting play, and responding by repeating the child's words or asking for clarification (Goldstein & Wickstrom, 1986). There is little information available on the use of peer-mediated interventions specifically with children with hearing impairment. Peer-mediated interventions have a solid history of success with children with various disabilities and should be considered an option for children with hearing impairment. If used in this way, confederate training would likely need to include instruction in sign language and/or in visual strategies for gaining the attention of the child with hearing impairment.

Another approach to supporting social integration for the child with hearing impairment is to orient peers to the needs and abilities of the deaf child. This should be approached with sensitivity and care: Evidence has shown that an intensive orientation approach can have an effect opposite of its intention, decreasing children's initiation toward children with hearing impairment (Vandell, Anderson, Ehrhart, & Wilson, 1982). An overly intense and focused approach may exaggerate the problems and differences generated by the disability. A more useful approach may be to focus less on the disability than on the child who has the disability, emphasizing his or her interests, strengths, and individual ways of coping successfully with the challenge of the disability. Books and ensuing discussions about communication, friendship, social relations, deaf culture, and characters with hearing impairment can be integrated throughout the curriculum, with accompanying attention to the many ways in which human beings are alike and different.

CHILDREN WITH AUTISM SPECTRUM DISORDERS

Autism Spectrum Disorders (ASD) refers to the broad category of "autism" and includes diagnoses of Aspergers, Autistic Disorder, and Pervasive Developmental Disorder. The common label of ASD has been used to identify these children (Gillberg, 1999). Decades ago, autism was first described as a triangle of features: extreme aloneness, a desire for sameness, and islets of ability (Kanner, 1943). This profile continues to characterize autism. As a spectrum disorder, the symptoms of autism can present themselves in a wide variety of combinations. Symptoms can range from mild to severe. Although autism is defined by a certain set of behaviors, there is no "typical" child with autism. While a specific cause of autism is not known, current research links autism to biological or neurological differences in the brain (Scott, Clark, & Brady, 2000).

Problems in social relatedness and reciprocity are central to the definition of ASD. Common features of ASD are impairments in social interaction and communication, and repetitive stereotyped patterns of behavior, interests, and activities. Frequent social problems associated with ASD include difficulty orienting to social stimuli, understanding facial expressions, responding to another's distress, using gaze to communicate, initiating interaction, using appropriate greetings, and establishing joint attention. Children with ASD often show impairments in spontaneous play and in initiation of pretend play (Weiss & Harris, 2001). They typically show little interest in peers, appear less socially engaged with peers, make and receive fewer initiations in peer interaction, and spend more time playing alone (Koegel, Koegel, Frea, & Fredeen, 2001).

Problems in reciprocal social exchange are a hallmark of ASD. Reciprocity is crucial to the development of social relationships. Therefore, interventions to promote social relatedness are a very important (and challenging) part of educating a child with ASD.

As with any child, identifying appropriate strategies for support and intervention for a child with ASD requires careful observation. Observational assessment can help determine particular skills and competencies the child needs to develop, as well as behaviors that should be replaced. Observing the antecedents and consequences that serve to elicit and maintain an undesirable behavior can be very useful. Knowledge of A-B-C analysis, as described earlier (see Sandall & Ostrosky, 1999 for further information), or functional assessment (see Chandler & Dahlquist, 2002) are useful tools to guide observation.

Successful strategies for enhancing the social engagement and social skills of children with ASD are often complex to administer, may require trained staff, and may involve focused intervention over a period of weeks to months. Most of the successful interventions are described in scientific journals; by necessity the details of implementation are generally very abbreviated in such publications. As with any disability, a collaborative team of professionals including individuals with good working knowledge of research-supported interventions can facilitate the inclusion of a child with ASD.

Early studies of social interventions for children with autism spectrum disorders involved adult-directed teaching, but it was generally observed that behaviors learned in this context did not generalize to the peer environment unless peers were also specifically trained. The research attention has shifted focus to interventions that involve peers from the start. Successful strategies involving peers have involved *typically developing* peers, as would be available in inclusive settings. Early inclusion in regular education environments has been shown to greatly assist in the learning of appropriate social responding and play behaviors for children with ASD (Kamps et al., 1992; Odom & Bailey, 2001).

A sampling of strategies that have been used to enhance the social engagement and/or social skills of children with ASD are briefly described below.

Script Training

Sociodramatic play is an important context for social interaction in the early childhood years. Children with ASD often have great difficulty engaging in spontaneous pretend play. Increased interaction can be created by structuring support for the child with ASD to be involved in sociodramatic play. This has been accomplished by training trios of children (two typically developing, one with autism) to enact sociodramatic play scripts. Each child practices each of the three roles involved in the script. For example, in a carnival script children can learn and enact the roles of game booth attendant, assistant, and customer. This type of approach has been shown to increase interaction during the script enactment, as well as to generalize to greater socialization during free play periods (Goldstein & Cisar, 1992; Goldstein, Wickstro, Hoyson, Jamieson, & Odom, 1988). For many teachers the notion of scripting dramatic play may seem intrusive and contrary to the view of this important kind of play as supporting self-expression, creativity, and imagination. It is important to remember that sociodramatic play can serve a wide variety of functions. Some children may need far more structured support to begin to access some of the most basic social benefits of social pretend play.

Individualized Interest Games

Another promising approach is for adults to create and teach games and social activities based on a child's "obsessive interests." Building upon children's individual interests is not a new notion to early childhood educators, and is recognized as one of the hallmarks of individually appropriate practice. Children with ASD are often characterized as having obsessive interests, displayed through preoccupation with particular objects, repeated patterns of movement, and idiosyncratic areas of information expertise (like detailed knowledge of all the kinds of furniture found in restaurants or all the kinds of ice cream made by Baskin-Robbins). For example, a teacher might design a social game for a 5-year-old who is obsessively interested in spinning the wheels on miniature toy cars. Such a game could involve using the cars as a substitute for a traditional game spinner (the teacher could mark colors or numbers at various points on the tire). By spinning a car wheel, children determine how many spaces to move on a simple board game. Research has demonstrated that high-functioning children with ASD can show dramatic increases in positive affect and peer interaction as a result of this simple type of intervention, and results generalize to other activities and are thus maintained (Baker, Koegel, & Koegel, 1998).

Peer-Mediated Approaches

Peer-mediated approaches were described in Chapter 6 as interventions in which the teacher or other professional trains peers to serve as confederates in the intervention. Because the individuals who intervene directly with the target child are peers, the need to develop procedures to transfer learning from adult partners to peer partners is eliminated. This factor appears to make important contribution to the effectiveness of peer-mediated interventions in general, and with children with autism in particular.

Peer-mediated approaches have been shown to be very powerful in increasing the social interactions of young children with autism. In typical peer-mediated interventions, peer confederates role-play with adults until they have learned the specified strategies. Then, in a natural context, the peer confederate is cued by the adult to interact with the child with ASD.

The adult reinforces the confederate for using the targeted strategies. This reinforcement is then gradually reduced.

Three basic types of peer-mediated approaches have been used: proximity, prompt/reinforce, and peer initiation approaches. In *proximity* interventions, peers are given no special training but are simply told to play with the child with autism; they may, for example, be told "do your best" to get the child with autism to play. An advantage of this approach is that it requires little facilitation by the teacher, and it has been shown to be effective in increasing the target child's social responsiveness and length of interactions. It has not, however, demonstrated a change in the rate of initiations by children with ASD (Roeyers, 1996).

Peer-initiation training teaches peers how to initiate toward a child with ASD. Peer confederates have been taught to initiate behaviors that serve as play organizers and to use these with the necessary perseverance. Such behaviors include sharing, helping, giving affection, praise, making requests, and asking questions. One intervention that taught peers to make comments to children with autism showed a very substantial increase in social behavior (Goldstein, Kaczmarek, Pennington, & Shafer, 1992). The open-ended nature of comments ("This tower is really getting tall"; "This is fun"; "You're making yours red, I'm making mine blue") does not demand a specific kind of response, and may therefore be easier for a child with autism to respond to and less likely to cause avoidance (a barrage of questions and requests could cause anyone to become avoidant).

Prompt/reinforcement training teaches peers to prompt social behavior by the child with autism and to reinforce the behavior when the child does it. For example, a teacher may train a peer confederate to say, "Look at this fun toy" while placing a social toy between them. The peer confederate is taught to reinforce by saying, "Good, you are looking," when joint attention to the play material is demonstrated. After this has been role-played several times with the teacher and mastered, the teacher cues the child to use the strategy with the target child and reinforces the peer confederate for doing so.

Peer-mediated approaches can be complex to deliver and usually require careful adult training of peer confederates, management of reinforcement of peer confederates, and monitoring of results. (For more detail about the specifics of implementing peer-mediated approaches, see Danko, Lawry, & Strain, 1998.)

Research suggests that sustainable, long-term positive social outcomes for children with autism require long-term, comprehensive, and intensive daily intervention and support (Strain & Hoyson, 2000). (For a resource on social interventions for children with ASD, see Koegel & Koegel, 1995.)

SUMMARY

When the classroom community includes a child with particular disabilities or particular social needs, a wide range of support and intervention strategies are available to the professionals working within that classroom. Decisions about intervention should be based on knowledge of the child, drawn from observation, and constructed through the collaboration of a team of appropriate individuals familiar with the child and with the nature of the child's disabilities. In general, the most normalized interventions, those requiring the least alteration to typical classroom functioning, should be considered first. Those interventions at the higher level of the hierarchy, which require the greatest resources and the most extensive changes to typical classroom routine, should be considered when more natural interventions have been deemed inadequate.

Children with particular disabilities often experience specific challenges to the development of their social competence. It is important to emphasize, however, that these may not be present for every child and will likely vary with the degree of severity of a child's disability. Nothing can substitute for knowledge of a unique individual child. Approaching Jimmy simply as "a child with autism," considering Audrey primarily as "a child with a hearing impairment," or categorizing Heather as "a shy child" may easily result in overlooking the true and essential nature of the individual child's strengths, capabilities, challenges, and needs.

Similarly, restricting choices only to those interventions described under a particular heading in this chapter would be a mistake. Much research, as well as practical wisdom, has supported the use of particular interventions for children with special needs. However, the literature is far from complete and far from comprehensive. To make the best decisions, teachers must rely on their knowledge of the individual child, child development, early childhood curriculum and teaching methods, and the intervention literature; on their own reflective capabilities; and on the support and collaboration of a team of professionals and parents representing multiple areas of experience and expertise regarding the child. The processes of reflective collaborative planning and practice, as described in Chapter 2, provide an important framework for selecting, implementing, evaluating, and modifying interventions to support young children's emerging social competence.

FOOD FOR THOUGHT

1. Children with Autism Spectrum Disorders are often characterized by a strong desire for sameness and predictability in their environment. Children with autism may be more tuned in to the precise physical charac-

teristics of their physical environment than are other children. They perceive slight alterations, and are often upset by even the smallest of changes. It has been suggested that their limited understanding of others' intentions and feelings and of interpersonal cause and effect make the constant flow and change of the social world hard for them to interpret. Consequently, they rely heavily on the predictability of routines and physical order to deal with an otherwise hyperunpredictable world (Schuler, 1995). Refer back to what you have read about physical environment, scheduling, and routines as supports for socially competent behavior. Create a list of 5 to 10 specific ways to help meet the need for sameness for a child with ASD.

2. Tuning curriculum, teaching, and social interventions to coincide with children's individual strengths and interests is an important feature of individually appropriate practice. Reflect back on the intervention and support methods described in this chapter. Consider how you might heighten the power of particular interventions by keying them to a child's individual assets. For example, a child who is deaf may arrive in your class already quite fluent in sign language. How could this special ability be used to enhance teaching basic signs to the rest of the children in the class? (The child with hearing impairment can do some of the teaching, of course!) Some shy children are very good observers of the social world; they may spend a lot of time in a wait-and-watch mode. For example, how could this individual feature be used to enhance, the use of group affection activities?

Closing Thoughts about Community and Collaboration

A
N ADULT VISITOR steps through the door of Room 3 and into the world of a kindergarten class. Near the entrance to the classroom are photographs taken during a recent cooperative pizza-making activity. Interspersed among photos are children's own comments and captions: A dictated "Pepperoni is the spiciest" and "first we put the sauce, then we sprinkled some cheese," and an inventive "I lik ptsa." On a wall opposite the door is a neat and proud display of children's individual artwork. This is not a collection of red, green, and brown construction paper apple trees. It is instead an assortment of self-selected masterpieces: a yarn picture of "my teacher," a pencil drawing of a house and swing set, a bright and bold marker representation of a rainbow, a collage of overlapping cuts of painted paper. On another wall, a low bulletin board has been arranged with a variety of child-created representations of "favorite things": puppies, cats, pizza, and [pictures of] people [who] have been created in various media by individual children and arranged in an amusing and imaginative way as the result of teacher-guided group effort.

On the floor, in a semicircular cluster, sit 20 kindergarteners and a teacher, Mrs. Starnes. A lively discussion is underway, on the topic of cleanup responsibilities. With facilitation by Mrs. Starnes, the children debate whether it is fair for some children to neglect to participate in the process of cleaning up after free-play time if they made no mess. This is clearly not an easily resolved moral dilemma. In the language of 5- and 6-year-olds, such issues are considered as these: Since the block area contains far more large individual pieces than does the book area, is it fair that children who happened to play with the blocks last should have to pick up a hundred blocks, while children who happened to read the books last have only a few items to replace? If I don't ever play with blocks, why should I have to help put them away? Can Ernie contribute to making an enormous mess in the block area, and then slip off to the book area 3 minutes before cleanup time?

The answers to these challenging queries are perhaps less important than the fact that these children are posing and considering them. The solution that the group ultimately agrees to is perhaps less important than the process they will go through to achieve it. Mrs. Starnes urges children to consider whether it is more important that everyone do exactly the same amount of work, whether it is more important that each child's cleanup effort be directed toward his or her own mess, or whether it is more important that their shared space be in functional and pleasing order. In this way, these young children consider important questions of fairness, individual rights, interdependence, and the value of community.

In *Habits of the Heart: Individualism and Commitment in American Life* (Bellah, Madsen, Sullivan, Swidler, & Tipton, 1985), the term *community* is defined as "a group of people who are socially interdependent, who participate together in discussion and decision-making, and who share certain practices that both define the community and are nurtured by it" (p. 333). In a society in which individualism is imbued with great value, the balance of community-building may present greater inherent tensions and challenges than in societies in which individualism is less exalted. Building a feeling of classroom community requires that children have an emergent understanding that they are a part of a larger entity, and that being cooperative and considerate of others' needs can benefit individual others, the entire group, and themselves (Howes & Ritchie, 2002). Individuals matter and so does the group.

The climate of Room 3 illustrates simultaneous nurturing of individuality and groupness. Those pieces of artwork attractively matted and displayed for all to see are creations of personal value to the artist. A group bulletin board display is the result of group process and collaboration, which pulls together individual efforts. Time is allowed for the valued process of making collaborative decisions about rules and procedures that affect the quality of community life.

Although I have not used the term *community building* throughout this book, the notion of building community is implicit in the combined themes of social inclusion, collaborative activity, and shared decision making within which I have organized my ideas and suggestions. To be an integrated participating member of the classroom community requires a degree of social capacity on the part of individual children, an attitude of invitation and acceptance on the part of the peer group, and flexibility and accommodation on the part of all. The creation of community is a goal of the process of promoting social competence. At the same time, the existence of community provides a nutrient culture in which social competence can grow. Healthy community is potentially both a means and an end to social competence.

Teaching practices that may serve to facilitate community building were briefly described in Chapter 3 as practices that communicate the following messages: this is a caring place; you belong here; we belong here. When a teacher-child relationship is characterized by trust, warmth, and caring, the young child can use the teacher as a secure base from which to explore peer relationships. This important base of security enables prosocial behavior among children, and hastens the development of community (Howes, & Ritchie, 2002). When teachers consciously work to support an ecology that recognizes each child as an individual and which is appreciative of each child's uniqueness, there is a message that each child matters and each child belongs. When teachers strive to support an atmosphere of "groupness" and explicitly value interdependence and cooperation, children hear the message, "We all belong here, and we belong here together." Community can grow when teachers convey the attitude and expectation that all participants (adults and children) have active responsibility for sustaining such a climate of caring, cooperation, and belonging.

Specific practices that can be used to encourage and sustain community include cooperative learning activities; collaborative investigation of problems of genuine interest; facilitated conversation and other forms of group process, such as voting, to address difficulties in classroom community life; circle times to celebrate classroom culture through sharing of favorite songs, stories, and rituals; frequent use of children's names and genuine incorporation of children's interests and affinities; shared responsibility for classroom care and beautification; meaningful visual documentations of shared history (class books, memory walls, calendar practices); and collaborative development and reassessment of the rules governing community life. Finally, the teaching and encouraging of all forms of prosocial behavior (helping, sharing, negotiating, comforting) conveys the message that everyone in the classroom (not only the adults) has responsibility for providing nurturance and working out problems.

In communities of strong professional collaboration, the same messages of caring and belonging are echoed: We are here working together because we care to do the best for children; we *each* belong because we each have something of value to contribute; we *all* belong, together, because no one of us has adequate knowledge or expertise alone. In collaborations that function well, the whole is far greater than the sum of its parts.

In a sense, a collaborative team of individuals who work to address the needs of individual children function, at least for a time, as a small community. The elements important to successful team collaboration (e.g. trust, respect, interdependence, joint problem-solving, and shared decision making) are the same elements that define a community of adults and children in an early childhood classroom.

Dispositions that contribute to successful professional collaboration include respect for individuals' professional expertise; willingness to share expertise; and readiness to release one's "hold" on expert knowledge and cross boundaries of job titles, professional hierarchies, and academic disciplines. Acceptance of individual differences, recognition of peers' special needs, respect for peers' special strength, and willingness to help and accommodate are dispositions that contribute to a successful and inclusive classroom community. The basic prosocial dispositions and skills that undergird successful team collaboration are those that support (and grow out of) a vital classroom community.

As professionals work together to address the social needs of young children, it may benefit us to reflect upon the similarity in the skills and dispositions we ourselves are required to exercise, as we engage in the process of planning to support children's successful community participation. A view of professionals engaged in a "community of practice" is a challenge to the one-directional model of "experts" and "novices." In a community of practice, we engage together in a process of inquiry toward a common goal. In a community of practice, we are all experts in some domain, just as we are all less skilled and less knowledgeable in others. As professionals work to help young children learn to hold hands, share, play fair, cooperate, and honor differences, we can be mindful to do the same.

Books for Children about Friendship and Friendship Skills

Agassi, M. (2000). *Hands are not for hitting*. Minneapolis: Free Spirit Publishing.

Bechtold, L. (1999). *Buster: The very shy dog*. Boston: Houghton Mifflin.

Berry, J. (1988). *A children's book about teasing*. Danbury, CT: Grolier Enterprises.

Bourgeois, P. (1997). *Franklin's new friend*. New York: Scholastic.

Bunnett, R. (1996). *Friends at school*. Long Island City, NY: Star Bright Books.

Burnett, K. G. (1999). *Simon's hook: A story about teases and put downs*. Felton, CA: GR Publishing.

Carlsson-Paige, N. (1998). *Best day of the week*. St. Paul, MN: Red Leaf Press.

Caseley, J. (1989). *Ada Potato*. New York: Greenwillow.

Chapman, C. (1981). *Herbie's troubles*. New York: Dutton.

Crary, E. (1992). *I'm frustrated (dealing with feelings)*. Seattle, WA: Parenting Press.

Crary, E. (1992). *I'm mad (dealing with feelings)*. Seattle, WA: Parenting Press.

Crary, E. (1996). *I can't wait*. Seattle, WA: Parenting Press.

Crary, E. (1996). *I want it*. Seattle, WA: Parenting Press.

Crary, E. (1996). *I want to play*. Seattle, WA: Parenting Press.

Crary, E. (1996). *My name is not Dummy*. Seattle, WA: Parenting Press.

Crary, E. (1996). *I'm furious (dealing with feelings)*. Seattle, WA: Parenting Press.

Crary, E. (1996). *When you're shy and you know it*. Seattle, WA: Parenting Press.

Cohen, M. (1989). *Will I have a friend?* New York: Aladdin.

Conlin, S., & Freedman, S. L. (1991). *All my feelings at preschool: Nathan's day*. Seattle, WA: Parenting Press.

Davies, S. (1999). *When William went away*. Minneapolis: Carolrhoda Books.

De Lynam, A. G. (1988). *It's mine*. New York: Dial.

DePaola, T. (1981). *Now one foot, now the other*. New York: Putnam.

Durrell, A., & Bierhorst, J. (1993). *The big book for peace*. New York: Dutton.

Everitt, B. (1992). *Mean soup*. San Diego: Harcourt, Brace, & Jovanovich.

Feldman, H. (2000). *My best friend: A book about friendship*. New York: Powerkids.

Gainer, C. (1998). *I'm like you, you're like me: A child's book about understanding and celebrating each other*. Minneapolis: Free Spirit Publishing.

Griffin, J. (1992). *Who is the boss?* New York: Houghton Mifflin.

Henkes, K. (1996). *Chrysanthemum*. Lancashire, UK: Mulberry Books.

Henkes, K. (1997). *Chester's way*. Lancashire, UK: Mulberry Books.

Henkes, K. (1998). *Jessica*. Lancashire, UK: Mulberry Books.

Jahn-Clough, L. (1999). *My friend and I*. Boston: Houghton Mifflin.

Jahn-Clough, L. (2001). *Simon and Molly plus Hester*. Boston: Houghton Mifflin.

Jones, R. (1991). *Matthew and Tilly*. New York: Dutton.

Kasza, K. (1993). *The rat and the tiger*. New York: Putnam.

Kent, S. (2000). *Let's talk about being a good friend*. New York: PowerKids.

Krauss, R. (2001). *I'll be you and you be me*. New York: HarperCollins.

Lalli, J. (1997). *I like being me: Poems for children about feeling special, appreciating others, and getting along*. Minneapolis: Free Spirit Publishing.

Levete, S. (1998). *Making friends*. Brookfield, CT: Copper Beech Books.

Levitin, S. (1991). *The man who kept his heart in a bucket*. New York: Dial.

Lionni, l. (1987). *Frederick*. New York: Knopf.

Lionni, L. (1992). *Swimmy*. New York: Knopf.

Lionni, L. (1999). *It's mine!* Minneapolis: Econo-clad Books.

Loh, M. (1990). *Tucking Mommy in*. London: Orchard Books.

Lucas, E. (1991). *Peace on the playground*. New York: Franklin Watts.

Marshall, J. (1974). *George and Martha*. Boston: Houghton Mifflin.

Merrifield, M. (1998). *Come sit by me*. Toronto: Stoddart Kids.

Naylor, P. R. (1991). *King of the playground*. New York: Atheneum.

Parr, T. (2000). *The best friends book*. Boston: Little, Brown.

Payne, L. M. (1994). *Just because I am: A child's book of affirmation*. Minneapolis: Free Spirit Publishing.

Payne, L. M., & Rohling, C. (1997). *We can get along: A child's book of choices*. Minneapolis: Free Spirit Publishing.

Pomerantz, C. (1998). *You're not my best friend anymore*. New York: Dial.

Rogers, F. M. (2001). *Extraordinary friends (Lets talk about it)*. New York: Puffin.

Rogers, F. M. (1996). *Making friends*. Paper Star.

Ross, D. (1999). *A book of friends*. New York: HarperCollins.

Scholes, K. (1990). *Peace begins with you*. San Francisco: Sierra Club Books.

Seuss, Dr. (1961). *The Sneetches and other stories*. London: Random House.

Seuss, Dr. (1984). *The butter battle book*. New York: Random House.

Sharmat, M. W. (1975). *I'm not Oscar's friend anymore*. New York: E. P. Dutton.

Spinelli, E. (1991). *Somebody loves you Mr. Hatch*. New York: Bradbury.

Steig, W. (1971). *Amos and Boris*. New York: Farrar, Strauss, & Giroux.

Steig, W. (1990). *Shrek!* Toronto: HarperCollins.

Stevens, J. (1993). *Coyote steals the blanket: A Ute tale*. New York: Holiday House.

Trumbauer, L., & Saunders-Smith, G. (2000). *Who is a friend?* Pebble Books.

Udry, J. M. (1961). *Let's be Enemies*. New York: Harper & Row.

Warburg, S. S. (1990). *I like you*. Boston: Houghton Mifflin.

Ward, S. (1991). *What goes around comes around*. New York: Doubleday.

Wells, R. (2001). *Shy Charles*. New York: Puffin.

Weninger, B. (1999). *Why are you fighting, Davy?* New York: North-South Books.

Whitman, S. (1978). *A special trade*. New York: Harper & Row.

Wyeth, S. D. (2002). *Something beautiful*. New York: Dragonfly.

Yaccarino, D. (2002). *Unlovable*. New York: Henry Holt.

Zolotow, C. (1982). *The quarreling book*. New York: HarperTrophy

Zolotow, C. (1989). *The hating book*. New York: HarperTrophy.

Zolotow, C. (2000). *My friend John*. New York: Doubleday.

Recorded Songs for Children That Address Social Topics

(Listed Alphabetically by Song Title)

SONGS ABOUT SOCIAL SKILLS

A friend like you. (1994). Penner, F. *What a day*. Winnipeg, Canada: Branch Group Music Publishing.

All work together. (1992). Guthrie, W., & Guthrie, A. *Woody's 20 grow big songs*. Dalton, MA: Warner Brothers Records, Inc.

Ask for it. (1982). Pelham, R. *Under one sky*. Albany, NY: Ruth Pelham Music.

Cheer up. (1994). Penner, F. *What a day*. Winnipeg, Canada: Branch Group Music Publishing.

Count to 10 and try again. (1998). Fink, C., & Marxer, M. *Changing channels*.

Don't you push me down. (1992). Guthrie, W., & Guthrie, A. *Woody's 20 grow big songs*. Dalton, MA: Warner Brothers Records, Inc.

Friends don't let friends. (1997). McCutcheon, J. *Bigger than yourself*. Cambridge, MA: Rounder Records Corp.

I got a dime. (1997). McCutcheon, J. *Bigger than yourself*. Cambridge, MA: Rounder Records Corp.

I know your face. (1982). Pelham, R. *Under one sky*. Albany, NY: Ruth Pelham Music.

I think you're wonderful. (1986). Grammer, R. *Teaching peace*. Brewerton, NY: Red Note Records.

Is not/is too. (1996). Fink, C., & Marxer, M. *Is not/is too* (video). Takoma Park, MD: Community Music.

Lean on me. (1994). Brodey, K., & Brody, J. *Like a ripple on the water*. Toronto: Casa Wroxton Studio.

Play fair. (1997). McCutcheon, J. *Bigger than yourself*. Cambridge, MA: Rounder Records Corp.

The principle. (1997). McCutcheon, J. *Bigger than yourself*. Cambridge, MA: Rounder Records Corp.

Say Hi! (1986). Grammer, R. *Teaching peace*. Brewerton, NY: Red Note Records.

Sharing. (1998). Fink, C., & Marxer, M. *Changing channels*. Cambridge, MA: Rounder Records.

The sharing song. (1976). Raffi. *Singable songs for the very young*. Vancouver, BC: Troubadour Records.

She's a baby. (1994). Penner, F. *What a day*. Winnipeg, Canada: Branch Group Music Publishing.

149

Someone else decide. (1997). McCutcheon, J. *Bigger than yourself*. Cambridge,
     MA: Rounder Records Corp.
Stick together. (1997). McCutcheon, J. *Bigger than yourself*. Cambridge, MA:
     Rounder Records Corp.
Take good care of each other. (1994). Penner, F. *What a day*. Winnipeg, Canada:
     Branch Group Music Publishing.
There are many ways to say I love you. (1994). Brodey, K., & Brody, J. *Like a
     ripple on the water*. Toronto: Casa Wroxton Studio.
Use a word. (1998). Fink, C., & Marxer, M. *Changing channels*. Cambridge, MA:
     Rounder Records.
Use a word. (1986). Grammer, R. *Teaching peace*. Brewerton, NY: Red Note Rec-
     ords.
Watcha gonna be? (1997). McCutcheon, J. *Bigger than yourself*. Cambridge, MA:
     Rounder Records Corp.
What do I do. (1982). Pelham, R. *Under one sky*. Albany, NY: Ruth Pelham Music.
Write it down. (1997). McCutcheon, J. *Bigger than Yourself*. Cambridge, MA:
     Rounder Records Corp.

SONGS ABOUT FRIENDSHIP AND COMMUNITY

A friend, a laugh, and a walk in the woods. (1992). Crow, D. *A friend, a laugh,
     and a walk in the woods*. New York: Sony Music.
A friend like you. (1994). Penner, F. *What a day*. Winnipeg, Canada: Branch Group
     Music Publishing.
A kid like me. (1994). Fink, C., & Marxer, M. *Nobody else like me*. Hollywood,
     CA: A&M Records.
Balanced on a giant web. (1994). Brodey, K., & Brodey, J. *Like a ripple on the
     water*. Toronto: Casa Wroxton Studio.
Bigger than yourself. (1997). McCutcheon, J. *Bigger than yourself*. Cambridge,
     MA: Rounder Records Corp.
Building a place. (1994). Brodey, K., & Brodey, J. *Like a ripple on the water*.
     Toronto: Casa Wroxton Studio.
Company coming. (1994). Penner, F. *What a day*. Winnipeg, Canada: Branch
     Group Music Publishing.
Family Garden. (1993). McCutcheon, J. *Family garden*. Cambridge, MA: Rounder
     Records.
Friends don't let friends. (1997). McCutcheon, J. *Bigger than yourself*. Cambridge,
     MA: Rounder Records Corp.
Friends. (1987). Greg & Steve. *On the move*. Los Angeles: YoungHeart Records.
Friendship. (1997). McCutcheon, J. *Bigger than yourself*. Cambridge, MA:
     Rounder Records Corp.
Happy adoption day. (1993). McCutcheon, J. *Family garden*. Cambridge, MA:
     Rounder Records.
Hello, Hello, Hello. (1994). Fink, C., & Marxer, M. *Nobody else like me*. Holly-
     wood, CA: A&M Records.

Hello, hello. (1982). Pelham, R. *Under one sky*. Albany, NY: Ruth Pelham Music.
How many people. (1993). McCutcheon, J. *Family garden*. Cambridge, MA: Rounder Records.
I belong. (1994). Brodey, K., & Brodey, J. *Like a ripple on the water*. Toronto: Casa Wroxton Studio.
I got a dime. (1997). McCutcheon, J. *Bigger than yourself*. Cambridge, MA: Rounder Records Corp.
I'll hold you. (1989). Atkinson, L. *The one and only me*. Albany, NY: A Gentle Wind.
Is my family. (1993). McCutcheon, J. *Family garden*. Cambridge, MA: Rounder Records.
It's such a good feeling. (1967). Rogers, F. *You are special*.
It's you I like. (1967). Rogers, F. *You are special*.
It takes a village. (2002). Raffi. *Let's play*! Vancouver, BC: Troubadour Records.
It takes a whole village to raise a child. (1994). Brodey, K., & Brodey, J. *Like a ripple on the water*. Toronto: Casa Wroxton Studio.
Love changes everything. (1998). Moo, A. *Makin' moosic*. Gainesville, FL: University of Florida.
Make new friends. (1996). Fink, C., & Marxer, M. *Is not/is too* (video). Takoma Park, MD: Community Music.
One light, one sun. (1990). Raffi. *Evergreen, everblue*. Vancouver, BC: Troubadour Records.
Simple thing. (1994). Brodey, K., & Brodey, J. *Like a ripple on the water*. Toronto: Casa Wroxton Studio.
Someone's gonna use it. (1990). Chapin, T. *Mother earth*. New York: Limousine Music Co. & The Last Music Co.
Stick together. (1997). McCutcheon, J. *Bigger than yourself*. Cambridge, MA: Rounder Records Corp.
Take good care of each other. (1994). Penner, F. *What a day*. Winnipeg, Canada: Branch Group Music Publishing.
The picnic of the world. (1990). Chapin, T. *Mother earth*. New York: Limousine Music Co. & The Last Music Co.
The world is our community. (1994). Brodey, K., & Brodey, J. *Like a ripple on the water*. Toronto: Casa Wroxton Studio.
Under one sky. (1982). Pelham, R. *Under one sky*. Albany, NY: Ruth Pelham Music.
We have each other. (1992). Paxton, T. *Suzy is a rocker*. New York: Sony Music.
When the rain comes down. (1994). Fink, C., & Marxer, M. *A Cathy & Marcy collection*. Takoma Park, MD: Community Music, Inc.
Won't you be my neighbor. (1967). Rogers, F. *Won't you be my neighbor*.
Write it down. (1997). McCutcheon, J. *Bigger than yourself*. Cambridge, MA: Rounder Records Corp.
You are my friend. (1998). Moo, A. *Makin' moosic*. Gainesville, FL: University of Florida.
You are special. (1967). Rogers, F. *You are special*.

SONGS ABOUT HONORING DIVERSITY

A little like you and a little like me. (1994). Fink, C., & Marxer, M. *Nobody else
like me*. Hollywood, CA: A&M Records.

Ballet-dancing truck driver. Fink, C., & Marxer, M. *Changing channels*. Cambridge, MA: Rounder Records.

Children all over the world. (1989). Atkinson, L. *The one and only me*. Albany,
NY: A Gentle Wind.

Different drums. (1994). Brodey, K., & Brodey, J. *Like a ripple on the water*.
Toronto: Casa Wroxton Studio.

Everybody has music inside. (1987). Greg & Steve. *We all live together Volume 4*.
Los Angeles: YoungHeart Records.

Everybody loves Saturday night. (1994). Brodey, K., & Brodey, J. *Like a ripple on
the water*. Toronto: Casa Wroxton Studio.

Everything possible. (1994). Fink, C., & Marxer, M. *Nobody else like me*. Hollywood, CA: A&M Records.

Family tree. (1988). Chapin, T. *Family tree*. New York: Limousine Music Inc. and
The Lat Music Co.

First peoples. (1994). Raffi. *Bananaphone*. Vancouver, BC: Troubadour Records.

Friendship. (1997). McCutcheon, J. *Bigger than yourself*. Cambridge, MA:
Rounder Records Corp.

Happy adoption day. (1993). McCutcheon, J. *Family garden*. Cambridge, MA:
Rounder Records.

Harry's glasses. (1994). Fink, C., & Marxer, M. *Nobody else like me*. Hollywood,
CA: A&M Records.

Hello, hello, hello. (1994). Fink, C., & Marxer, M. *Nobody else like me*. Hollywood, CA: A&M Records.

I belong. (1994). Brodey, K., & Brodey, J. *Like a ripple on the water*. Toronto:
Casa Wroxton Studio

I see with my hands. (1994). Fink, C., & Marxer, M. *Nobody else like me*. Hollywood, CA: A&M Records.

I'm proud of you. (1970). Rogers, F. *Coming and going*.

Its great being me. (1994). Penner, F. *What a day*. Winnipeg, Canada: Branch
Group Music Publishing.

Like me and you. (1985). Raffi. *One light, one sun*. Vancouver, BC: Troubadour
Records.

My name is Daniel. (1990). Hartmann, J. *Make a friend, be a friend*. Freeport, NY:
Activity Records, Inc.

Nobody else like me. (1994). Fink, C., & Marxer, M. *Nobody else like me*. Hollywood, CA: A&M Records.

Seeing with my ears. (1982). Pelham, R. *Under one sky*. Albany, NY: Ruth Pelham
Music.

Special kids. (1994). Fink, C., & Marxer, M. *Nobody else like me*. Hollywood,
CA: A&M Records.

The world is our community. (1994). Brodey, K., & Brodey, J. *Like a ripple on the
water*. Toronto: Casa Wroxton Studio.

To everyone in all the world. (1980). Raffi. *Baby beluga*. Vancouver, BC: Trouba-
  dour Records.
Walkin' on my wheels. (1994). Fink, C., & Marxer, M. *Nobody else like me*.
  Hollywood, CA: A&M Records.
When the rain comes down. (1994). Fink, C., & Marxer, M. *A Cathy & Marcy
  collection*. Takoma Park, MD: Community Music, Inc.
You are special. (1967). Rogers, F. *You are special*.

References

Alberto, P. A., & Troutman, A. C. (1990). *Applied behavior analysis for teachers* (3rd Ed.). Columbus, OH: Merrill.

Almy, M., & Genishi, C. (1979). *Ways of studying children.* New York: Teachers College Press.

American Psychological Association (1993). *Violence and youth: Psychology's response Volume I summary report of the American Psychological Association Commission on Violence and Youth.* Washington, DC: Author.

Antia, S. D. (1982). Social interaction of partially mainstreamed hearing impaired children. *American Annals of the Deaf, 127*(1), 18–25.

Antia, S. (1994). Strategies to develop peer interaction in young hearing-impaired children, *Volta Review, 96*(4), 277–290.

Antia, S. D., & Kreimeyer, K. H. (1992). Social competence intervention for young children with hearing impairments. In Odom, S. L., McConnell, S. R., & McEvoy, M. A. (Eds.), *Social competence of young children with disabilities: Issues and strategies for intervention.* Baltimore: Paul H. Brookes.

Antia, S. D., Kreimeyer, K. H., & Eldredge, N. (1993). Promoting social interaction between young children with hearing impairments and their peers. *Exceptional Children, 60*(3), 262–275.

Asher, S. R. (1990). Recent advances in the study of peer rejection. In S. Asher and J. Coie (Eds.), *Peer rejection in childhood* (pp. 3–14). New York: Cambridge University Press.

Baker, M. J., Koegel, R. L., & Koegel, L. K. (1998). Increasing the social behavior of young children with autism using their obsessive behaviors. *Journal of the Association for Persons with Severe Handicaps, 23*(4), 300–308.

Beckman, P. J., & Kohl, F. L. (1984). The effects of social and isolate toys on the interactions and play of integrated and nonintegrated groups of preschoolers. *Education and Training of the Mentally Retarded, 22,* 169–174.

Bellah, R. N., Madsen, R., Sullivan, W. M., Swidler, A., & Tipton, S. M. (1985). *Habits of the heart: Individualism and commitment in American life.* Berkeley, CA: University of California Press.

Bergen, D. (1994). *Assessment methods for infants and toddlers: Transdisciplinary team approaches.* New York: Teachers College Press.

Bernat, V. (1993). Teaching peace. *Young Children, 48*(3), 36–39.

Birch, S. H., & Ladd, G. W. (1996). Interpersonal relationships in the school environment and children's early school adjustment: The role of teachers and peers. In K. W. Wentzel & J. H. Juvonen (Eds.), *Social motivation: Understanding children's school adjustment*. New York: Cambridge University Press.

Blaska, J. K. (1996). *Using children's literature to learn about disabilities and illness*. Moorhead, MN: Practical Press.

Blaska, J. K., & Lynch, E. C. (1998). Is everyone included? Using children's literature to facilitate the understanding of disabilities. *Young Children, 53*(2), 36–38.

Bodrova, E., & Leong, D. (1996). *Tools of the mind: The Vygotskian approach to early childhood education*. Upper Saddle River, NJ: Merrill/Prentice-Hall.

Boyer, E. L. (1990). *Ready to learn: A mandate for the nation*. Princeton, NJ: The Carnegie Foundation for the Advancement of Teaching.

Boyer, E. L. (1995). *The basic school: A community for learning*. Princeton, NJ: Carnegie Foundation for the Advancement of Teaching.

Bredekamp, S. (1987). *Developmentally appropriate practice in early childhood programs serving children birth through age eight*. Washington, DC: National Association for the Education of Young Children.

Bredekamp, S. (1993). The relationship between early childhood education and early childhood special education: Healthy marriage or family feud? *Topics in Early Childhood Special Education, 13*(3), 258–273.

Bredekamp, S., & Copple, C. (1997). *Developmentally appropriate practice in early childhood programs* (Rev. ed.). Washington, DC: National Association for the Education of Young Children.

Bricker, D. (1989). *Early intervention for at-risk and handicapped infants, toddlers, and preschool children*. Palo Alto, CA: VORT.

Bricker, D., Pretti-Frontczak, K., & McComas, N. (1998). *An activity-based approach to early intervention*. Baltimore: Paul H. Brookes.

Brown, M. H., Althouse, R., & Anfin, C. (1993). Guided dramatization: Fostering social development in children with disabilities. *Young Children, 48*(2), 68–71.

Brown, W. H., & Conroy, M. A. (1997). Promoting and supporting peer interaction in inclusive classrooms: Effective strategies for early childhood educators. In W. H. Brown & M. A. Conroy (Eds.), *Inclusion of preschool children with developmental delays in early childhood programs* (pp. 79–108). Little Rock, AR: Southern Early Childhood Association.

Brown, W. H., Fox, J. J., & Brady, M. P. (1987). The effects of spatial density on the socially directed behavior of three and four-year-old children during freeplay: An investigation of a setting factor. *Education and Treatment of Children, 10*, 247–258.

Brown, W. H., & Odom, S. L. (1994). Strategies and tactics for promoting generalization and maintenance of young children's social behavior. *Research in Developmental Disabilities, 15*(2), 99–118.

Brown, W. H., & Odom, S. L. (1995). Naturalistic peer interventions for promoting preschool children's social interactions. *Preventing School Failure, 39*, 38–43.

Brown, W. H., Odom, S. L., & Conroy, M. A. (2001). An intervention hierarchy for promoting preschool children's peer interactions in naturalistic environments. *Topics in Early Childhood Special Education, 21*(3), 162–175.

Brown, W. H., Ragland, G. G., & Fox, J. J. (1988). Effects of group socialization procedures on the social interactions of preschool children. *Research in Developmental Disabilities, 9,* 359–376.

Bruder, M. B. (1994). Working with members of other disciplines: Collaboration for success. In M. Wolery & J. S. Wilbers (Eds.), *Including children with special needs in early childhood programs.* Washington, DC: National Association for the Education of Young Children.

Bryant, D., Vizzard, L. H., Willoughby, M., & Kupersmidt, J. (1999). A review of interventions for preschoolers with aggressive and disruptive behavior. *Early Education and Development, 10*(1), 47–68.

Bunnett, R., & Davis, N. L. (1997). Getting to the heart of the matter. *Child Care Information Exchange, 114,* 42–44.

Cameron, J., & Pierce, W. D. (1996). The debate about rewards and intrinsic motivation: A meta-analysis. *Review of Educational Research, 64*(3), 363–423.

Carlsson-Paige, N., & Levin, D. E. (1992a). Moving children from time-out to win-win. *Child Care Information Exchange, 84,* 38–42.

Carlsson-Paige, N., & Levin, D. (1992b). Making peace in violent times: A constructivist approach to conflict resolution. *Young Children, 48*(1), 4–12.

Carta, J. (1995). Developmentally appropriate practice: A critical analysis as applied to young children with disabilities. *Focus on Exceptional Children, 27*(8), 1–14.

Carta, J. J., Atwater, J. B., Schwartz, I. S., & McConnell, S. R. (1993). Developmentally appropriate practices and early childhood special education: A reaction to Johnson & McChesney Johnson. *Topics in Special Education, 13,* 243–254.

Carta, J. J., Schwartz, I. S., Atwater, J. B., & McConnell, S. R. (1991). Developmentally appropriate practice: Appraising its usefulness for young children with disabilities. *Topics in Early Childhood Special Education, 11*(1), 1–20.

Chandler, L. (1998). Promoting positive interaction between preschool-age children during free play: The PALS center. *Young Exceptional Children, 1*(3), 14–19.

Chandler, L., & Dahlquist, C. M. (1993). *The PALS center: Strategies to promote peer social interaction.* Poster presented at the Applied Behavior Analysis and Behavior Analysis Society of Illinois Conference, Chicago, IL.

Chandler, L., & Dahlquist, C. M. (2002). *Functional assessment: Strategies to prevent and remediate challenging behavior in school settings.* Upper Saddle River, NJ: Merrill.

Chandler, L., Fowler, S. A., & Lubeck, R. C. (1992). An analysis of the effects of multiple setting events on the social behavior of preschool children with special needs. *Journal of Applied Behavior Analysis, 25,* 249–263.

Chandler, L., Lubeck, R. C., & Fowler, S. A. (1992). Generalization and maintenance of preschool children's social skills: A critical review and analysis. *Journal of Applied Behavior Analysis, 25,* 415–428.

Charlesworth, R., & Hartup, W. W. (1967). Positive social reinforcement in the nursery school peer group. *Child Development, 38,* 993–1002.

Christie, J. F., & Wardle, F. (1992). How much time is needed for play? *Young Children, 47*(2), 28–32.

Clarke, B. K. (1985). Bibliotherapy through puppetry: Socializing the young child can be fun! *Early Child Development and Care, 19,* 337–344.

Clements, R. (2001). *Elementary school recess.* Boston: American Press.

Cohen, E. G. (1994). Restructuring the classroom: Conditions for productive small groups. *Review of Educational Research, 64*(1), 1–35.

Cohen, D. H., Stern, V., & Balaban, N. (1997). *Observing and recording the behavior of young children* (4th ed.). New York: Teachers College Press.

Committee for Children. (2002). *Second step: A violence prevention curriculum, preschool-kindergarten.* Seattle, WA: Committee for Children.

Conroy, M. A., & Brown, W. H. (in press). Promoting peer-related social-communicative competence in preschool children with developmental delays. In H. Goldstein, L. Kaczmarek, & K. M. English (Eds.), *Promoting social communication in children and youth with developmental disabilities.* Baltimore: Paul H. Brookes.

Conroy, M. A., Langenbrunner, M. R., & Burleson, R. B. (1996, Winter). Suggestions for enhancing the social behaviors of preschoolers with disabilities using developmentally appropriate practices. *Dimensions of Early Childhood,* 9–15.

Conroy, M. C., & Brown, W. H. (2002). Preschool children: Putting research into practice. In H. Goldstein, L. A. Kaczmarek & K. M. English (Eds.), *Promoting social communication: Children with developmental disabilities from birth to adolescence.* Baltimore, Paul H. Brookes.

Correa, V., Hartle, L., Jones, H., Kemple, K., Rapport, M. J., & Smith-Bonahue, T. (1997). The Unified ProTeach Early Childhood Program at the University of Florida. In L. Blanton, C. Griffin, J. Winn, & M. Pugach (Eds.), *Teacher education in transition: Collaborative practices in general and special education.* (pp. 84–105). Denver, CO: Love Publishing.

Crary, E. (1984). *Kids can cooperate: A practical guide to teaching problem-solving.* Seattle, WA: Parenting Press.

Danko, C. D., Lawry, J., & Strain, P. S. (1998). *Social skills intervention manual packet.* Unpublished manuscript.

DeKlyen, M., & Odom, S. L. (1989). Structure and preschool social interactions: Beyond the mainstream. *Journal of Early Intervention, 13,* 342–353.

Denham, S., & Almeida, M. (1987). Children's social problem-solving skills, behavioral adjustment, and interventions: A meta-analysis evaluating theory and practice. *Journal of Applied Developmental Psychology, 8,* 391–409.

Dewey, J. (1933). *How we think.* Chicago: Henry Regnery Company.

DeWolfe, M., & Benedict, J. (1997). Social development and behavior in the integrated curriculum. In C. H. Hart, D. C. Burts, & R. Charlesworth (Eds.), *Integrated curriculum and developmentally appropriate practice: Birth to age eight.* Albany, NY: State University of New York Press.

Diamond, K. E., Hestenes, L. L., Carpenter, E. S., & Innes, F. K. (1997). Relationships between enrollment in an inclusive class and preschool children's ideas about people with disabilities. *Topics in Early Childhood Special Education, 17*(4), 520–536.

Dinwiddie, S. A. (1994). The saga of Sally, Sammy, and the red pen: Facilitating children's social problem-solving. *Young Children, 49*(5), 13–19.

Dodge, K. A., & Crick, N. R. (1990). Social information-processing bases of aggressive behavior in children. *Personality and Social Psychology Bulletin, 16*, 8–22.

Duncan, T., Kemple, K. M., & Smith, T. (2000). Developmentally appropriate practice and the use of reinforcement in inclusive early childhood classrooms. *Childhood Education, 76*(4), 194–203.

Educational Productions (1987a). *Between you and me: Facilitating child-child conversations* [Video]. Educational Productions.

Educational Productions (1987b). *Good talking with you: Language acquisition through conversation* [Video Series]. Educational Productions.

Edwards, C. (1992). Creating safe places for conflict resolution to happen. *Child Care Information Exchange, 84*, 43–45.

Eisenberger, R., & Cameron, J. (1996). Detrimental effects of reward: Reality or myth. *American Psychologist, 51*(11), 1153–1166.

English, K., Goldstein, H., Shafer, K., & Kaczmarek, L. (1997). Promoting interactions among preschoolers with and without disabilities: Effects of a buddy skills training program. *Exceptional Children, 63*, 229–243.

Favazza, P. C., & Odom, S. L. (1997). Promoting positive attitudes of kindergarten-age children toward people with disabilities. *Exceptional Children, 63*(3), 405–418.

File, N. K. (1993). The teacher as a guide of children's competence with peers. *Child and Youth Care Forum, 22*(5), 351–360.

File, N. K. (1994). Children's play, teacher-child interaction, and teacher beliefs in integrated early childhood programs. *Early Childhood Research Quarterly, 9*, 223–240.

Gareau, M., & Kennedy, C. (1991). Structure time and space to promote pursuit of learning in the primary grades. *Young Children, 46*(4), 46–51.

Gillberg, C. (1999). Prevalence of disorders in the autism spectrum. *Infants and Young Children, 10*, 64–74.

Glendinning, C. (1995). Recovery from western civilization. In G. Sessions (Ed.), *Deep ecology for the 21st century*. Boston: Shambala.

Goldstein, H., & Cisar, C. L. (1992). Promoting interaction during sociodramatic play: Teaching scripts to typical preschoolers and classmates with disabilities. *Journal of Applied Behavior Analysis, 25*, 265–280.

Goldstein, H., English, K., Shafer, K., & Kaczmarek, L. (1997). Interaction among preschoolers with and without disabilities: Effects of across-the-day peer intervention. *Journal of Speech, Language, and Hearing Research, 40*, 33–48.

Goldstein, H., Kaczmarek, L., Pennington, R., & Shafer, K. (1992). Peer-mediated intervention: Attending to, commenting on, and acknowledging the behavior of preschoolers with autism. *Journal of Applied Behavior Analysis, 25*(2), 289–305.

Goldstein, H., & Wickstrom, S. (1986). Peer intervention effects on communicative interaction among handicapped and nonhandicapped preschoolers. *Journal of Applied Behavior Analysis, 19*(2), 209–214.

Goldstein, H., Wickstrom, S., Hoyson, M., Jamieson, B., & Odom, S. (1988). Effects of sociodramatic play training on social and communicative interaction. *Education and Treatment of Children, 11,* 97–117.

Goleman, D. (1995). *Emotional intelligence: Why it can matter more than IQ.* New York: Bantam Books.

Gonzalez-Mena, J. (1993). *Multicultural issues in child care.* Mountainview, CA: Mayfield.

Gonzalez-Mena, J. (1997). *Multicultural issues in child care.* Mountainview, CA: Mayfield Publishing.

Greenberg, M. T., & Kusche, C. A. (1993). *Promoting social and emotional development in deaf children: The PATHS Project.* Seattle, WA: University of Washington Press.

Guralnick, M. J. (1990). Social competence and early intervention. *Journal of Early Intervention, 14,* 3–14.

Guralnick, M. J. (1993). Developmentally appropriate practice in the assessment and intervention of children's peer relations. *Topics in Early Childhood Special Education, 13*(3), 344–371.

Guralnick, M. J. (1999). The nature and meaning of social integration for young children with mild developmental delays in inclusive settings. *Journal of Early Intervention, 22*(1), 70–86.

Guralnick, M. J., Gottman, J. M., & Hammond, M. A. (1996). Effects of social setting on the friendship formation of young children differing in developmental status. *Journal of Applied Developmental Psychology, 17,* 625–651.

Guralnick, M. J., & Groom, J. M. (1988). Friendships of preschool children in mainstreamed playgroups. *Developmental Psychology, 24*(4), 595–604.

Guralnick, M. J., & Neville, B. (1997). Designing early intervention programs to promote children's social competence. In M. J. Guralnick (Ed.), *The effectiveness of early intervention* (pp. 579–610). Baltimore: Paul H. Brookes.

Gutkin, T. B., & Curtis, M. J. (1982). School-based consultation: Theory and techniques. In C. R. Reynolds & T. B. Gutkin (Eds.), *The handbook of school psychology* (pp. 796–828). New York: Wiley.

Hart, B., & Risley, T. R. (1980). In vivo language intervention: Unanticipated general effects. *Journal of Applied Behavior Analysis, 13,* 407–432.

Hartup, W. W. (1983). Peer relations. In M. Heatherington (Ed.), *Handbook of child psychology* (Vol. 4, pp. 103–196). New York: Wiley.

Hartup, W., & Moore, S. G. (1991). Early peer relations: Developmental significance and prognostic implications. *Early Childhood Research Quarterly, 5,* 1–7.

Hazen, N. L., Black, B., & Fleming-Johnson, F. (1984). Social acceptance: Strategies children use and how teachers can help children learn them. *Young Children, 39*(6), 26–36.

Henderick, J. (1998). *Total learning: Developmental curriculum for the young child.* Columbus, OH: Merrill.

Hendrickson, J. M., Strain, P. S., Tremblay, A., & Shores, R. E. (1981). Relationship between toy and material use and the occurrence of social interactive behaviors by normally developing preschool children. *Psychology in the Schools, 18*, 50–55.

Honig, A. S. (1987). The shy child. *Young Children 42*(4), 54–64.

Howe, N. (1993). The ecology of dramatic play centers and children's social and cognitive play. *Early Childhood Research Quarterly, 8*, 235–251.

Howes, C., & Hamilton, C. (1993). The changing experience in child-care: Changes in teachers and teacher-child relations and children's social competence with peers. *Early Childhood Research Quarterly, 8*, 15–32.

Howes, C., & Ritchie, S. (2002). *A matter of trust: Connecting teachers and learners in the early childhood classroom.* New York: Teachers College Press.

Hymel, S., Wagner, E., & Butler, L. J. (1990). Reputational bias: View from the peer group. In S. Asher & J. Coie (Eds.), *Peer rejection in childhood* (pp. 156–186). New York: Cambridge University Press.

Hyson, M. C. (1994). *The emotional development of young children: Building an emotion-centered curriculum.* New York: Teachers College Press.

Idol, L. (1993). *Special educator's consultation handbook (2nd ed).* Austin, TX: PRO-ED.

Jalongo, M. R. (1983). Using crisis-oriented books with young children. *Young Children, July*, 29–36.

Jalongo, M. R., & Stamp, L. (1997). *The arts in children's lives: Aesthetic education in early childhood.* Boston: Allyn & Bacon.

Johnson, D., & Johnson, R. (1991). *Learning together and alone: Cooperative, competitive, and individualistic learning.* Englewood Cliffs, NJ: Prentice-Hall.

Jones, E., & Nimmo, J. (1999). Collaboration, conflict, and change: Thoughts on education as provocation. *Young Children, 54*(1), 5–10.

Kagan, S. L. (1991). *United we stand: Collaboration in child care and early education services.* New York: Teachers College Press.

Kamps, D. M., Leonard, B. R., Vernon, S., Dugan, E. P., Delquadri, J. C., Gershon, B., Wade, L., & Folk, L. (1992). Teaching social skills to students with autism to increase peer interactions in an integrated first-grade classroom. *Journal of Applied Behavior Analysis, 25*, 281–288.

Kanner, L. (1943). Autistic disturbances of affective contact. *Nervous Child, 2*, 217–240.

Katz, L. G., & McClellan, D. E. (1997). *Fostering children's social competence: The teacher's role.* Washington, DC: National Association for the Education of Young Children.

Kazdin, A. E. (1994). *Behavior modification in applied settings.* Pacific Grove, CA: Brooks/Cole.

Kemple, K., David, G., & Hysmith, C. (1997). Teachers' interventions in young children's peer interactions. *Journal of Research in Childhood Education, 12*(1), 34–47.

Kemple, K., & Hartle, L. (1999). Getting along: How teachers can support children's peer relationships. *Annual Editions in Early Childhood Education* (4th ed., pp. 130–137). Guildford, CT: Dushkin/McGraw Hill.

Kemple, K., Hartle, L., Correa, V., & Fox, L. (1994). Preparing teachers for inclusive education: The development of a unified teacher education program in early childhood and early childhood special education. *Teacher Education and Special Education, 17*(1), 38–51.

Kinsman, C., & Berk, L. (1979). Joining the block and housekeeping areas: Changes in play and social behavior. *Young Children, 35*(7), 66–75.

Knopczyk, D. R., & Rodes, P. G. (1996). *Teaching social competence: A practical approach for improving social skills for students.* Pacific Grove, CA: Brookes/Cole.

Koegel, R. L., & Koegel, L. K. (1995). *Teaching children with autism: Strategies for initiating positive interactions and improving learning opportunities.* Baltimore: Paul H. Brookes.

Koegel, L. K., Koegel, R. L., Frea, W. D., & Fredeen, R. M. (2001). Identifying early intervention targets for children with autism in inclusive school settings. *Behavior Modification, 25*(5), 745–761.

Kohl, F. L., & Beckman, P. J. (1984). A comparison of handicapped and nonhandicapped preschoolers' interactions across classroom activities. *Journal of the Division of Early Childhood, 8,* 49–56.

Kohler, F. W., & Strain, P. S. (1990). Peer-assisted interventions: Early promises, notable achievements, and future aspirations. *Clinical Psychology Review, 22,* 441–454.

Kohler, F. W., & Strain, P. S. (1999). Maximizing peer-mediated resources in integrated preschool classrooms. *Topics in Early Childhood Special Education, 19*(2), 92–102.

Kohn, A. (1993). *Punished by rewards: The trouble with gold stars, incentive plans, A's, praise, and other bribes.* New York: Houghton Mifflin.

Kontos, S., & File, N. (1993). The relationship of program quality to children's play in integrated early intervention settings. *Topics in Early Childhood Special Education, 13*(1), 1–18.

Kontos, S., & Wilcox-Herzog, A. (1997). Influences on children's competence in early childhood classrooms. *Early Childhood Research Quarterly, 12*(3), 247–262.

Kostelnik, M. J., Soderman, A. K., & Whiren, A. P. (1999). *Developmentally appropriate curriculum: Best practices in early childhood education.* Upper Saddle River, NJ: Merrill.

Kostelnik, M. J., & Stein, L. C. (1990). Social development: An essential component of kindergarten education. In J. S. McKee (Ed.), *The developing kindergarten: Programs, children, and teachers.* Saginaw, MI: Mid-Michigan Association for the Education of Young Children.

Kostelnik, M. J., Stein, L. C., Whiren, A. P., & Soderman, A. K. (1998). *Guiding children's social development.* Cincinnati, OH: South-Western.

Kostelnik, M. J., Whiren, A. P., Soderman, A. K., Stein, L. C., & Gregory, K. (2002). *Guiding children's social development: Theory to practice.* Albany, NY: Delmar.

Kreidler, W. J. (1984). *Creative conflict resolution: More than 200 activities for keeping peace in the classroom.* Glencoe, IL: Scott, Foresman & Company.

Krogh, S. L., & Lamme, L. L. (1985). "But what about sharing?": Children's literature and moral development. *Young Children, 40*(4), 48–51.

Kupersmidt, J. B., Coie, J. D., & Dodge, K. A. (1990). The role of poor peer relationships in the development of disorder. In S. R. Asher & J. D. Coie (Eds.), *Peer rejection in childhood* (pp. 274–305). New York: Cambridge University Press.

Kusche, C. A., & Greenberg, M. T. (1989). Cortical organization and information processing in deaf children. In D. Martin (Ed.), *Advances in cognition, education and deafness.* Washington, DC: Gallaudet University Press.

Ladd, G. W., & Coleman, C. C. (1997). Children's classroom peer relationships and early school attitudes: Concurrent and longitudinal associations. *Early Education and Development, 8*(1), 51–66.

Ladd, G. W., & Coleman, C. C. (1993). Young children's peer relationships: Forms, features, and functions. In B. Spodek (Ed.), *Handbook of research on the education of young children* (pp. 54–76). New York: MacMillan.

Ladd, G. W., & Kochenderfer, B. J. (1996, April). *Classroom peer acceptance, friendship, and victimization: Distinct relational systems that contribute uniquely to children's school adjustment.* Paper presented at the American Educational Research Association Meetings, New York.

Lamme, L. L., & McKinley, L. (1992). Creating a caring classroom with children's literature. *Young Children, 48*(1), 65–71.

Lazar, I., Darlington, R., Murray, H., Royce, J., & Snipper, A. (1982). Lasting effects of early education. *Monographs of the Society for Research in Child Development (No. 194).* Chicago: University of Chicago Press.

Lee, V. B. (1939). *Mike Mulligan and his steam shovel.* Boston: Houghton-Mifflin.

Lepper, M. R., & Greene, D. (1975). When two rewards are worse than one: Effects of extrinsic rewards on intrinsic motivation. *Phi Delta Kappan, 56*(8), 565–566.

Lieber, J., Beckman, P. J., Hanson, M. J., Janko, S., Marquart, J. M., Horn, E., & Odom, S. L. (1997). The impact of changing roles on relationship between professionals in inclusive programs for young children. *Early Education and Development, 8,* 67–82.

Lowenthal, B. (1992). Collaborative training in the education of early childhood educators. *Teaching Exceptional Children, 24*(4), 25–29.

Luetke-Stahlman, B. (1994). Procedures for socially integrating preschoolers who are hearing, deaf, and hard of hearing. *Topics in Early Childhood Special Education, 14*(4), 472–487.

Mallory, B. (1994). Inclusive policy, practice, and theory for young children with developmental differences. In B. Mallory & R. New (Eds.), *Diversity and developmentally appropriate practices: Challenges for early childhood education.* New York: Teachers College Press.

Malmskog, S., & McDonnell, A. P. (1999). Teacher-mediated facilitation of engagement by children with developmental delays in inclusive preschools. *Topics in Early Childhood Special Education, 19*(4), 203–216.

Marion, M. (1992). *Guidance of young children.* (3rd ed.). New York: MacMillan.

Maslow, A. H. (1954). *Motivation and personality*: New York: Harper & Row.

McEvoy, M. A., Fox, J. J., & Rosenberg (1991). Organizing preschool environments: Suggestions for enhancing the development/learning of preschool children with handicaps. *Topics in Early Childhood Special Education, 11*(2), 18–28.

McEvoy, M. A., Nordquist, V. M., Twardosz, S., Heckaman, K., Wehby, J. H., & Denny, R. K. (1988). Promoting autistic children's peer interaction in an integrated early childhood setting using affection activities. *Journal of Applied Behavior Analysis, 21*, 193–200.

McEvoy, M. A., Odom, S. L., & McConnell, S. R. (1992). Peer social competence intervention for young children with disabilities. In S. Odom, S. McConnell, & M. McEvoy (Eds.), *Social competence of young children with disabilities: Issues and strategies for intervention* (pp. 113–133). Baltimore: Paul H. Brookes.

McEvoy, M. A., Twardosz, S., & Bishop, N. (1990). Affection activities: Procedures for encouraging young children with handicaps to interact with their peers. *Education and Treatment of Children, 13*, 159–167.

McGinnis, E., & Goldstein, A. P. (1990). *Skill-streaming in early childhood: Teaching prosocial skills to the preschool and kindergarten child*. Champaign, IL: Research Press.

McGinnis, E., & Goldstein, A. P. (1997). *Skillstreaming the elementary school child: New Strategies and perspectives for teaching prosocial skills*. (Rev. Ed.). Champaign, IL (ERIC Document Reproduction Service No. ED 416 609)

McGinnis, E., & Goldstein, A. P. (1999). *Skillstreaming the elementary school child: New strategies and perspectives for teaching prosocial skills*. Champaign, IL. Research Press.

McGregor, G., & Vogelsberg, R. T. (1998). *Inclusive schooling practices: Pedagogical and research foundations; a synthesis of the literature that informs best practices about inclusive schooling*. Baltimore: Paul H. Brookes.

Meers, J. (1985). The light touch. *Psychology Today, 19*(9), 60–67.

Miller, P. S. (1992). Segregated programs of teacher education in early childhood: Immoral and inefficient practice. *Topics in Early Childhood Special Education, 11*, 39–52.

Mize, J. (1995). Coaching preschool children in social skills: A cognitive social learning curriculum. In G. Cartledge and J. F. Milburn (Eds.), *Teaching social skills to children and youth: Innovative approaches*. (3rd ed., 237–261). Boston, MA: Allyn & Bacon.

Mize, J., & Ladd, G. W. (1990). A cognitive-social learning approach to social skills training with low status preschool children. *Developmental Psychology, 26*(3), 388–397.

Mize, J., Ladd, G. W., & Price, J. M. (1985). Promoting positive peer relations with young children: Rationales and strategies. *Child Care Quarterly, 14*, 221–237.

Moore, G. T. (1996). A question of privacy: Places to pause and child caves. *Child Care Information Exchange, 112*, 91–95.

National Association for the Education of Young Children (1995).

National Association for the Education of Young Children and the National Association of Early Childhood Specialists in State Departments of Education (1991). Guidelines for appropriate curriculum content and assessment in programs serving children ages 3 through 8. *Young Children, 46*(3), 21–38.

National Head Start Association (1990). Head Start: The nation's pride, a nations challenge. The final report of the Silver Ribbon Panel. *National Head Start Association Journal, 8*(4).

Neilsen, S., Olive, M., Donovan, A., & McEvoy, M. A. (1999). Challenging behaviors in your classroom? In S. Sandall & M. Ostrosky (Eds.), *Practical ideas for addressing challenging behaviors.* Denver, CO: Division of Early Childhood (DEC).

Niemeyer, J. A., & McEvoy, M. A. (1990, October). *Affection activities: Procedures for teaching young children at-risk for abuse to interact.* Paper presented at the annual conference of the Division for Early Childhood, Albuquerque, NM.

Odom, S. L., & Bailey, D. (2001). Inclusive preschool programs: Classroom ecology and child outcomes. In M. J. Guralnick (Ed.), *Early childhood inclusion: Focus on change* (pp. 253–276). Baltimore: Paul H. Brookes.

Odom, S. L., & Brown, W. H. (1993). Social interaction skill interventions for young children with disabilities in integrated settings. In C. Peck, S. Odom, & D. Bricker, (Eds.), *Integrating young children with disabilities into community programs* (pp. 39–64). Baltimore: Paul H. Brookes.

Odom, S. L., Chandler, L., Ostrosky, M., McConnell, S. R., & Reaney, S. (1992). Fading teacher prompts from peer-initiation interventions for young children with disabilities. *Journal of Applied Behavior Analysis, 25,* 307–318.

Odom, S. L., & Diamond, K. F. (1998). Inclusion of young children with special needs in early childhood education: The research base. *Early Childhood Research Quarterly, 13*(1), 3–25.

Odom, S. L., & McConnell, S. R. (1993). *Play time/social time: Organizing your classroom to build interaction skills.* Tucson, AZ: Communications Skill Builders.

Odom, S. L., McConnell, S. R., & Chandler, L. K. (1993). Acceptability and feasibility of classroom-based social interaction interventions for young children with disabilities. *Exceptional Children, 60,* 226–236.

Odom, S. L., McConnell, S. R., & McEvoy, M. A. (Eds.). (1992). *Social competence of young children with disabilities: Nature, development, and intervention.* Baltimore: Paul H. Brookes.

Odom, S. L., McConnell, S. R., & McEvoy, M. A. (1999). Relative effects of interventions supporting the social competence of young children with disabilities. *Topics in Early Childhood Education, 19*(2), 75–91.

Odom, S. L., & McLean, M. E. (1996). *Early intervention/early childhood special education: Recommended practices.* Austin, TX: PRO-Ed.

Odom, S. L., Peterson, C., McConnell, S., & Ostrosky, M. (1990). Ecobehavioral analysis of early childhood special education classroom settings and peer social interaction. *Education and Treatment of Children, 13*(4), 316–330.

Odom, S., & Strain, P. S. (1986). A comparison of peer-initiation and teacher ante-cedent interventions for promoting reciprocal social interaction of autistic pre-schoolers. *Journal of Applied Behavior Analysis, 19,* 59–72.

Odom, S. L., Zercher, C., Marquart, J., Li, S., Sandall, S. R., & Wolfberg, P. (2002). Social relationships of children with disabilities and their peers in in-clusive preschool classrooms. In S. L. Odom, (Ed.), *Widening the circle: In-cluding children with disabilities in preschool programs.* New York: Teachers College Press.

Okagaki, L., Diamond, K. E., Kontos, S. J., & Hestenes, L. L. (1998). Correlates of young children's interactions with classmates with disabilities. *Early Child-hood Research Quarterly, 13*(1), 67–86.

Oken-Wright, P. (1992). From tug of war to let's make a deal: The teacher's role. *Young Children, 48*(1), 15–20.

Olds, A. R. (1989). Psychological and physiological harmony in child care design. *Children's Environments Quarterly, 6*(4), 8–16.

O'Shaughnessy, E. (1992). *Somebody called me a retard today . . . and my heart felt sad.* New York: Walker & Company.

Parker, J. G., & Asher, S. R. (1987). Peer relations and later personal adjustment: Are low accepted children at risk? *Psychological Bulletin, 102,* 357–389.

Parten, M. B. (1933). Social play among preschool children. *Journal of Abnormal and Social Psychology, 28,* 136–147.

Patterson, G. R., & White, G. D. (1970). It's a small world: The application of time out from reinforcement. In F. H. Kanfer & J. S. Phillips (Eds.), *Learning foundations of behavior therapy.* New York: Wiley.

Pepler, D., & Slaby, R. G. (1994). Theoretical and developmental perspectives on youth and violence. In L. D. Aron, J. H. Gentry, & P. Schlegel (Eds.), *Reason to hope: A psychosocial perspective on violence and youth.* Washington, DC: American Psychological Association.

Perry, J. P. (2001). *Outdoor play: Teaching strategies with young children.* New York: Teachers College Press.

Peterson, C., McConnell, S., Cronin, P., Spicuzza, R., & Odom, S. (1991). *Child-specific intervention manuals.* Unpublished curriculum manual, Vanderbilt-Minnesota Social Interaction Project, John F. Kennedy Center, Vanderbilt University, Nashville, TN.

Piaget, J. (1963). *The origins of intelligence in children.* New York: Norton.

Prescott (1984). The physical setting in day care. In J. Greenman (Ed.), *Making day care better.* New York: Teachers College Press.

Proshansky, H. M., & Fabian, A. K. (1987). Development of place identity in the child. In C. S. Weinstein & T. G. David (Eds.), *Spaces for children: The built environment and child development* (pp. 21–40). New York: Plenum Press.

Quay, L. C., Weaver, J. H., & Neel, J. H. (1986). The effects of play materials on positive and negative social behaviors in preschool boys and girls. *Child Study Journal, 16*(1), 67–76.

Quilitch, H. R., & Risley, T. R. (1973). The effects of play materials on social play. *Journal of Applied Behavior Analysis, 6,* 573–578.

Raffi, Pike, D., Simpson, B., & Simpson, B. (1976). The Sharing Song. On *Singable songs for the very young* (1). Vancouver, BC, Canada: Homeland Publishing/ SOCAN, A division of Troubadour Records.

Rainforth, B., York, J., & McDonald, C. (1992). *Collaborative teams for students with severe disabilities: Integrating therapy and educational services.* Baltimore: Paul H. Brookes.

Ramsey, P. G. (1991). *Making friends in school: Promoting peer relationships in early childhood.* New York: Teachers College Press.

Rankin, B. (1997). Education as collaboration: Learning from and building on Dewey, Vygotsky, and Piaget. In J. Hendrick (Ed.), *First steps toward teaching the Reggio way.* Upper Saddle River, NJ: Merrill.

Rettig, M., Kallam, M., & McCarthy-Salm, K. (1993). The effect of social and isolate toys on the social interactions of preschool-aged children. *Education and Training in Mental Retardation, 28,* 252–256.

Rodd, J. (1996). *Understanding young children's behavior: A guide for early childhood professionals.* New York: Teachers College Press.

Roeyers, H. (1996). The influence of nonhandicapped peers on the social interactions of children with a pervasive developmental disorder. *Journal of Autism and Developmental Disorders, 26,* 303–320.

Rogers, S. J. (2000). Interventions that facilitate socialization in children with autism. *Journal of Autism and Developmental Disorders, 30*(5), 399–409.

Rogers, S. J., & Puchalski, C. B. (1984). Social characteristics of visually impaired infants' play. *Topics in Early Childhood Special Education, 3*(4), 52–56.

Rogers-Warren, A. K. (1977). Planned change: Ecobehaviorally based interventions. In A. K. Rogers-Warren & S. F. Warren (Eds.), *Ecological perspectives in behavior analysis* (pp. 197–210). Baltimore: University Park Press.

Rogoff, B. (1990). *Apprenticeship in thinking: Cognitive development in social context.* New York: Oxford University Press.

Ross, D. D., Bondy, E., & Kyle, D. W. (1993). *Reflective teaching for student empowerment: Elementary curriculum and methods.* New York: Macmillan.

Rubin, K. H. (1977). The social and cognitive value of preschool toys and activities. *Canadian Journal of Behavioral Science, 9,* 382–385.

Rubin, K. H., & Asendorf, J. (1993). *Social withdrawal, inhibition and shyness in childhood.* Hillsdale, NJ: Erlbaum.

Rubin, K. H., Bukowski, W., & Parker, J. (1998). Peer interactions, relationships, and groups. In N. Eisenberg (Ed.), *Handbook of Child Psychology: Social and Emotional Development* (Vol. 3, pp. 619–700). New York: Wiley.

Rubin, K. H., & Rose-Krasnor, L. (1992). Interpersonal problem-solving. In V. Van Hasselt & M. Hersen (Eds.), *Handbook of social development,* (pp. 283–324). New York: Plenum.

Russell-Fox, J. (1997). Together is better: Specific tips on how to include children with various types of disabilities. *Young Children, 52*(4) 81–83.

Sainato, D. M., & Carta, J. J. (1992). Classroom influences on the development of social competence in young children with disabilities. In S. Odom, S. McConnell, & M. McEvoy (Eds.), *Social competence of young children with disabili-*

ties: Issues and strategies for intervention (pp. 93–109). Baltimore: Paul H. Brookes.

Sandall, S., & Ostrosky, M. (1999). *Practical ideas for addressing challenging behavior.* Denver, CO: DEC.

Schloss, P. J., & Smith, M. A. (1998). *Applied behavior analysis in the classroom* (Rev. ed.). Boston: Allyn & Bacon.

Schneider, B. H., & Byrne, B. M. (1985). Children's social skills training: A meta-analysis. In B. Schneider, K. H. Rubin, & J. Ledingham (Eds.), *Children's peer relations: Issues in assessment and intervention* (pp. 3–22). New York: Springer-Verlag.

Schon, D. A. (1983). *The reflective practitioner.* New York: Basic Books.

Schuler, A. L. (1995). Thinking in autism: Differences in learning and development. In K. A. Quill (Ed.), *Teaching children with autism: Strategies to enhance communication and socialization.* New York: Delmar.

Schweinhart, L. J., Weikart, D. P., & Larner, M. B. (1986). Consequences of three preschool curriculum models through age 15. *Early Childhood Research Quarterly, 1,* 15–45.

Scott, J., Clark, C., & Brady, M. P. (2000). *Students with autism: Characteristics and instructional programming for special educators.* San Diego, CA: Singular Publishing Group.

Shure, M. (1992). *I can problem-solve: An interpersonal cognitive problem solving program.* Champaign, IL: Research Press.

Skellenger, A. C., Hill, M. M., & Hill, E. (1992). The social functioning of children with visual impairments. In Odom, S. L., McConnell, S. R., & McEvoy, M. A. (Eds.), *Social competence of young children with disabilities: Issues and strategies for intervention.* Baltimore: Paul H. Brookes.

Slaby, R. G., Roedell, W. C., Arezzo, D., & Hendrix, K (1995). *Early violence prevention: Tools for teachers of young children.* Washington, DC: National Association for the Education of Young Children.

Smith, P., & Connolly, K. (1980). *The ecology of preschool behavior.* Cambridge, UK: Cambridge University Press.

Stein, L. C., & Kostelnik, M. J. (1984). A practical problem-solving model for conflict resolution in the classroom. *Child Care Quarterly, 13*(1), 5–20.

Stoneman, Z., Cantrell, M. L., & Hoover-Dempsey, K. (1983). The association between play materials and social behavior in a mainstreamed preschool: A naturalistic investigation. *Journal of Applied Developmental Psychology, 4,* 163–174.

Strain, P. S., & Fox, J. J. (1981). Peer social initiations and the modification of social withdrawal: A review and future perspective. *Journal of Pediatric Psychology, 6,* 417–433.

Strain, P. S., & Hoyson, M. (2000). The need for longitudinal, intensive social skill intervention: LEAP follow-up outcomes for children with autism. *Topics in Early Childhood Special Education,* 116–122.

Strain, P. S., & Shores, R. E. (1983). A reply to "Misguided Mainstreaming." *Exceptional Children, 50,* 271–272.

Sulzer-Azaroff, B., & Mayer, G. R. (1991). *Behavior analysis for lasting change.* New York: Harcourt-Brace.

Swallow, W. K. (2000). *The shy child: Helping children triumph over shyness.* New York: Warner Books.

Tegano, D. W., & Burdette, M. (1991). Length of activity periods and play behaviors of preschool children. *Journal of Research in Childhood Education, 5*(2), 93–99.

Thomas, C. C., Correa, V. I., & Morsink, C. V. (2001). *Interactive teaming: Enhancing programs for students with special needs.* Upper Saddle River, NJ: Merrill.

Thomas, S. B., & Russo, C. J. (1995). *Special education law: Issues and implications for the 90's.* Topeka, KS: National Organization on Legal Problems of Education.

Trawick-Smith, J. (1990). The classroom affects children's play and development. *Dimensions of Early Childhood, 20*(2), 27–30, 40.

Tudge, J., & Caruso, D. (1988). Cooperative problem-solving in the classroom: Enhancing young children's cognitive development. *Young Children, 44*(1), 46–52.

Twardosz, S., Nordquist, V. M., Simon, R., & Botkin, D. (1983). The effects of group affection activities on the interaction of socially isolated children. *Analysis and Intervention in Developmental Disabilities, 3,* 311–338.

Udry, J. M. (1961). *Let's be enemies.* New York: Harper & Row.

Van Alstyne, D. (1932). *Play behavior and choice of play materials of preschool children.* Chicago: University of Chicago Press.

Vandell, D. L., Anderson, L. D., Ehrhart, G., & Wilson, K. S. (1982). Integrating hearing and deaf preschoolers: An attempt to enhance hearing children's interactions with deaf peers. *Child Development, 53,* 1354–1363.

Vandell, D. L., & Corasaniti, M. A. (1990). Variations in early child care: Do they predict subsequent social, emotional, and cognitive differences. *Early Childhood Research Quarterly, 5,* 555–572.

Vandell, D. L., Henderson, V. K., & Wilson, K. S. (1988). A longitudinal study of children with varying quality child care experiences. *Child Development, 59,* 1286–1292.

Vandercook, T., & York, J. (1990). A team approach to program development and support. In S. Stainback & W. Stainback (Eds.), *Support networks for inclusive schooling.* Baltimore: Paul H. Brookes.

Vaughn, S., Bos, C. S., & Schumm, J. S. (1997). *Teaching mainstreamed, diverse, and at-risk students in the general education classroom.* Boston: Allyn & Bacon.

Vygotsky, L. S. (1978). *Mind in society: The development of psychological processes.* Cambridge, MA: Harvard University Press.

Wasserman, S. (2000). *Serious players in the primary classroom.* (2nd ed.). New York: Teachers College Press.

Weinstein, C. S. (1987). Designing preschool classrooms to support development. In C. S. Weinstein & T. G. David (Eds.), *Spaces for children: The built environment and child development* (pp. 159–181). New York: Plenum Press.

Weiss, M. J., & Harris, S. L. (2001). Teaching social skills to people with autism. *Behavior Modification, 25*(5), 785–802.

West, J. F., & Cannon, G. S. (1988). Essential collaborative consultation competencies for regular and special educators. *Journal of Learning Disabilities, 21,* 56–63.

Wolery, M. (1994a). Assessing children with special needs. In M. Wolery & J. S. Wilbers (Eds.), *Including Children with Special Needs in Early Childhood Programs* (pp. 71–96). Washington, DC: National Association for the Education of Young Children.

Wolery, M. (1994b). *Including children with special needs in early childhood programs.* Washington, DC: National Association for the Education of Young Children.

Wolery, M., Ault, M. J., & Doyle, P. M. (1992). *Teaching students with moderate and severe disabilities: Use of response prompting strategies.* White Plains, NY: Longman.

Wolery, M., & Bredekamp, S. (1994). Developmentally appropriate practices and young children with disabilities: Contextual issues in the discussion. *Journal of Early Intervention, 18,* 331–341.

Wolery, M., Strain, P. S., & Bailey, D. B. (1992). Reaching potentials of children with special needs. In S. Bredekamp & T. Rosegrant (Eds.), *Reaching potentials: Appropriate curriculum and assessment for young children* (Vol. 1, pp. 92–111). Washington, DC: NAEYC.

Wolery, M., Werts, M. G., & Holcombe-Ligon, A. (1994). Current practices with young children who have disabilities: Issues in placement, assessment and instruction. *Focus on Exceptional Children, 26*(6), 1–12.

Wolery, M., & Wilbers, J. S. (1994). Introduction to the inclusion of young children with special needs in early childhood programs. In M. Wolery & J. S. Wilbers (Eds.), *Including Children with Special Needs in Early Childhood Programs* (pp. 1–22). Washington, DC: National Association for the Education of Young Children.

Wolfe, M. (1978). Childhood and privacy. In I. Altman & J. F. Wohlwill (Eds.), Children and the environment (pp. 175–222). New York: Plenum.

Yoshikawa, H. (1994). Prevention as cumulative protection: Effects of early family support and education on chronic delinquency and its risks. *Psychological Bulletin, 115*(1), 28–54.

Zirpoli, T. J. (1995). *Understanding and affecting the behavior of young children.* Englewood Cliffs, NJ: Merrill.

Index

About the Author

KRISTEN MARY KEMPLE is an associate professor in the School of Teaching and Learning at the University of Florida. She holds a Ph.D. in child development and family relationships, an M.A. in child development, and a B.A. in linguistics, all from the University of Texas at Austin. Dr. Kemple has taught and supervised in a variety of early childhood programs. She is a member of the faculty of the Unified ProTeach Early Childhood Program, a 5-year collaborative cross-departmental program designed to prepare professionals to work with diverse children from birth to age 8 in inclusive settings. Dr. Kemple's research and writing focus on the development of social competence in early childhood, as well as on creativity and the arts in early education.